Cyrus Thomas

Notes on certain Maya and Mexican manuscripts

Cyrus Thomas

Notes on certain Maya and Mexican manuscripts

ISBN/EAN: 9783742830210

Manufactured in Europe, USA, Canada, Australia, Japa

Cover: Foto ©ninafisch / pixelio.de

Manufactured and distributed by brebook publishing software
(www.brebook.com)

Cyrus Thomas

Notes on certain Maya and Mexican manuscripts

SMITHSONIAN INSTITUTION——BUREAU OF ETHNOLOGY

NOTES

ON CERTAIN

MAYA AND MEXICAN MANUSCRIPTS.

BY

PROF. CYRUS THOMAS.

3-4

CONTENTS.

ILLUSTRATIONS.

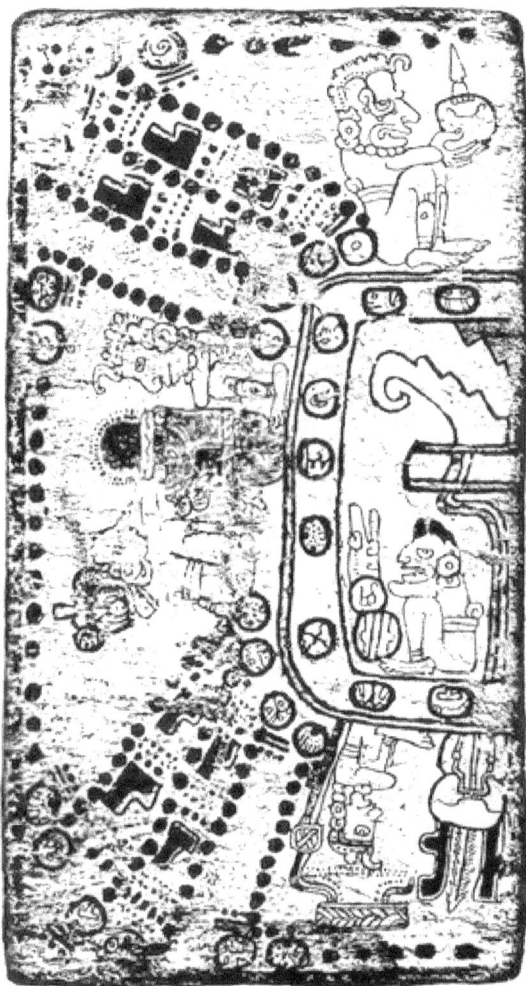

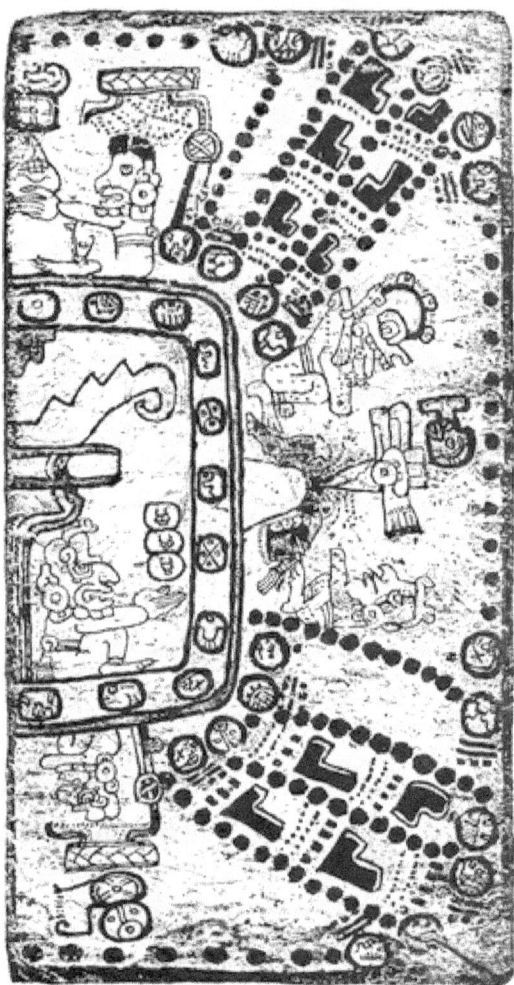

CODEX CORTESIANUS.

NOTES ON CERTAIN MAYA AND MEXICAN MANU-SCRIPTS.

By Cyrus Thomas.

"TABLEAU DES BACAB."

Having recently come into possession of Leon de Rosny's late work, entitled "*Les Documents ecrits de l'Antiquite Americaine*,"[1] I find in it a photo-lithographic copy of two plates (or rather one plate, for the two are but parts of one) of the Maya Manuscript known as the *Codex Cortesianus*. This plate (I shall speak of the two as one) is of so much importance in the study of the Central American symbols and calendar systems that I deem it worthy of special notice; more particularly so as it furnishes a connecting link between the Maya and Mexican symbols and calendars.

This plate (Nos. 8 and 9 in Rosny's work), is entitled by Rosny "*Tableau des Bacab*" or "Plate of the Bacabs," he supposing it to be a representation of the gods of the four cardinal points, an opinion I believe to be well founded.

As will be seen by reference to our Plate No. 1, which is an exact copy from Rosny's work, this page consists of three divisions: *First*, an inner quadrilateral space, in which there are a kind of cross or sacred tree; two sitting figures, one of which is a female, and six characters. *Second*, a narrow space or belt forming a border to the inner area, from which it is separated by a single line; it is separated from the outer space by a double line. This space contains the characters for the twenty days of the Maya month, but not arranged in consecutive order. *Third*, an outer and larger space containing several figures and numerous characters, the latter chiefly those representing the Maya days. This area consists of two distinct parts, one part containing day characters, grouped together at the four corners, and connected by rows of dots running from one group to the other along the outer border; the other part consisting of four groups of figures, one group opposite each of the four sides. In each of the four compartments containing these last-mentioned groups, there is one of the four characters shown in Fig. 1 (*a b c d*), which, in my "Study of the Manuscript Troano," I have concluded represent the four cardinal points, a conclusion also reached independently by Rosny and Schultz Sellack.

[1] Published in 1882, as a memoir of the Société d'Ethnographie of Paris.

Before entering upon the discussion of this plate I will insert here Rosny's comment, that the reader may have an opportunity of comparing his view of its signification with the opinion I shall advance.

I intend to close this report with some observations on the criticisms which have been written since the publication of my " Essay on the Decipherment of the Hieratic Writings," as much regarding the first data, for which we are indebted to Diego de Landa, as that of the method to follow in order to realize new progress in the interpretation of the Katounic texts. I will be permitted, however, before approaching this discussion, to say a word on two leaves of the *Codex Cortesianus*, which not only confirm several of my former lectures, but which furnish us probably a more than ordinarily interesting document relative to the religious history of ancient Yucatan.

The two leaves require to be presented synoptically, as I have done in reproducing them on the plate [8 and 9[1]], for it is evident that they form together one single representation.

This picture presents four divisions, in the middle of which is seen a representation of the sacred tree; beneath are the figures of two personages seated on the ground and placed facing the katounes, among which the sign of the day *Ik* is repeated three times on the right side and once with two other signs on the left side. The central image is surrounded by a sort of framing in which have been traced the twenty cyclic characters of the calendar. Some of these characters would not be recognizable if one possessed only the data of Landa, but they are henceforth easy to read, for I have had occasion to determine, after a certain fashion, the value of the greater part of them in a former publication.

These characters are traced in the following order, commencing, for example, with Muluc and continuing from left to right : 6, 2, 18, 13, 17, 14, 5, 1, 16, 12, 8, 4, 20, 15, 11, 7, 19, 3, 9, 10.   *   *   *

In the four compartments of the Tablet appear the same cyclic signs again in two series. I will not stop to dwell upon them, not having discovered the system of their arrangement.

Besides these cyclic signs no other katounes are found on the Tablet, except four groups which have attracted my attention since the beginning of my studies, and which I have presented, not without some hesitation, as serving to note the four cardinal points. I do not consider my first attempt at interpretation as definitely demonstrated, but it seems to me that it acquires by the study of the pages in question of the *Codex Cortesianus*, a new probability of exactitude.

These four katounic groups are here in fact arranged in the following manner :

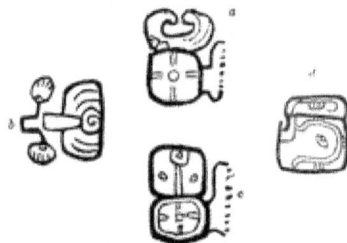

Fig. 1.—The four cardinal symbols.

Now, not only do these groups include, as I have explained, several of the phonetic elements of Maya words known to designate the four cardinal points, but they oc-

[1] Rosny says by mistake "Planche VII-VIII."

cupy, besides, the place which is necessary to them in the arrangement (orientation), to wit:

West.

South.

North.

East.

I have said, moreover, in my Essay, that certain characteristic symbols of the gods of the four cardinal points (the Bacab) are found placed beside the katounic groups, which occupy me at this moment, in a manner which gives a new confirmation of my interpretation.

On Plates 23, 24, 25, and 26 of the Codex Cortesianus, where the same groups and symbols are seen reproduced of which I have just spoken, the hierogrammat has drawn four figures identical in shape and dress. These four figures represent the "god of the long nose." Beside the first, who holds in his hand a flaming torch, appears a series of katounes, at the head of which is the sign Kan (symbol of the south), and above, a defaced group. Beside the second, who holds a flaming torch inverted, is the sign Mulue (symbol of the east), and above, the group which I have interpreted as east. At the side of the third, who carries in the left hand the burning torch inverted and a scepter (symbol of Bacabs), is the sign Ix (symbol of the north), and above, the group which I have translated as north. Finally, beside the fourth, who carries in his left hand the flaming torch inverted and a hatchet in the right hand, is the sign Cauac (symbol of the west), and above, not the entire group, which I have translated as west, but the first sign of this group, and also an animal characteristic of the Occident, which has been identified with the armadillo. I have some doubts upon the subject of this animal, but its affinity with the qualification of the west appears to me at least very probable.

We see from this quotation that Rosny was unable to give any explanation of the day characters, dots, and L-shaped symbols in the outer space; also that he was unable to suggest any reason for the peculiar arrangement of the day symbols in the intermediate circle or quadrilateral. His suggestions are limited to the four characters placed opposite the four sides, and which, he believes, and I think correctly, to be the symbols of the four cardinal points. Whether his conclusion as to the points they respectively refer to be correct or not, is one of the questions I propose to discuss in this paper. But before entering upon this, the most important question regarding the plate, I desire first to offer what I believe will be admitted to be a correct explanation of the object and uses of the day symbols, dots, &c., in the outer space, and the intermediate circle of day characters.

If we examine carefully the day characters and large black dots in the outer space we shall find that all taken together really form but one *continuous line*, making one outward and two inward bends or loops at each corner.

For example, commencing with *Cauac* (No. 31) (see scheme of the plate, Fig. 2), on the right side, and running upward toward the top along the row of dots next the right-hand margin, we reach the character *Chuen* (No. 32); just above is *Eb* (No. 33); then running inward toward the center, along the row of dots to * Kan* (No. 34); then upward to *Chicchan* (No. 35); then outward along the row of dots toward the outer corner to *Caban* (No. 36); then to the left to *Ezanab* (No. 37); then inward to *Oc* (No. 38); then to the left to *Chuen* (No. 39); outward to *Akbal* (No. 40), and so on around.

Before proceeding further it is necessary that I introduce here a Maya calendar, in order that my next point may be clearly understood. To simplify this as far as possible, I give first a table for a single *Cauac* year, in two forms, one as the ordinary counting-house calendar (Table I), the other a simple continuous list of days (Table II), but in this latter case only for thirteen months, just what is necessary to complete the circuit of our plate.

As explained in my former paper,[1] although there were twenty days in each Maya month, each day with its own particular name, and always following each other in the same order, so that each month would begin with the same day the year commenced with, yet it was the custom to number the days up to 13 and then commence again with 1, 2, 3, and so on, thus dividing the year into weeks of thirteen days each.

For a full explanation of this complicated calendar system I must refer the reader to my former paper. But at present we shall need only an understanding of the tables here given. I shall, as I proceed, refer to Table I, leaving the reader who prefers to do so to refer to the list of days marked Table II, as they are precisely the same thing, only differing in form.

TABLE I.—*Maya calendar for one year*

Nos. of the months.	1	2	3	4	5	6	7	8	9	10	11	12	13	14	15	16	17	18
Cauac	1	8	2	9	3	10	4	11	5	12	6	13	7	1	8	2	9	3
Ahau	2	9	3	10	4	11	5	12	6	13	7	1	8	2	9	3	10	4
Ymix	3	10	4	11	5	12	6	13	7	1	8	2	9	3	10	4	11	5
Ik	4	11	5	12	6	13	7	1	8	2	9	3	10	4	11	5	12	6
Akbal	5	12	6	13	7	1	8	2	9	3	10	4	11	5	12	6	13	7
Kan	6	13	7	1	8	2	9	3	10	4	11	5	12	6	13	7	1	8
Chicchan	7	1	8	2	9	3	10	4	11	5	12	6	13	7	1	8	2	9
Cimi	8	2	9	3	10	4	11	5	12	6	13	7	1	8	2	9	3	10
Manik	9	3	10	4	11	5	12	6	13	7	1	8	2	9	3	10	4	11
Lamat	10	4	11	5	12	6	13	7	1	8	2	9	3	10	4	11	5	12
Muluc	11	5	12	6	13	7	1	8	2	9	3	10	4	11	5	12	6	13
Oc	12	6	13	7	1	8	2	9	3	10	4	11	5	12	6	13	7	1
Chuen	13	7	1	8	2	9	3	10	4	11	5	12	6	13	7	1	8	2
Eb	1	8	2	9	3	10	4	11	5	12	6	13	7	1	8	2	9	3
Been	2	9	3	10	4	11	5	12	6	13	7	1	8	2	9	3	10	4
Ix	3	10	4	11	5	12	6	13	7	1	8	2	9	3	10	4	11	5
Men	4	11	5	12	6	13	7	1	8	2	9	3	10	4	11	5	12	6
Cib	5	12	6	13	7	1	8	2	9	3	10	4	11	5	12	6	13	7
Caban	6	13	7	1	8	2	9	3	10	4	11	5	12	6	13	7	1	8
Ezanab	7	1	8	2	9	3	10	4	11	5	12	6	13	7	1	8	2	9

TABLE II.

1st Month.	6. Kan.	12. Oc.	5. Cib.
1. Cauac.	7. Chicchan.	13. Chuen.	6. Caban.
2. Ahau.	8. Cimi.	1. Eb.	7. Ezanab.
3. Imix.	9. Manik.	2. Been.	2D Month.
4. Ik.	10. Lamat.	3. Ix.	8. Cauac.
5. Akbal.	11. Muluc.	4. Men.	9. Ahau.

[1] A study of the Manuscript Troano.

10. Ymix.	2. Chicchan	7. Muluc.	12. Been.
11. Ik.	3. Cimi.	8. Oc.	13. *Ix.*
12. Akbal.	4. Manik.	9. Chuen.	1. *Men.*
13. *Kan.*	5. Lamat.	10. Eb.	2. Cib.
1. *Chicchan.*	6. Muluc.	11. Been.	3. Caban.
2. Cimi.	7. Oc.	12. Ix.	4. Ezanab.
3. Manik.	8. Chuen.	13. *Men.*	9TH MONTH.
4. Lamat.	9. Eb.	1. *Cib.*	5. Canac.
5. Muluc.	10. Been.	2. Caban.	6. Ahau.
6. Oc.	11. Ix.	3. Ezanab.	7. Ymix.
7. Chuen.	12. Men.	7TH MONTH.	8. Ik.
8. Eb.	13. *Cib.*	4. Canac.	9. Akbal.
9. Been.	1. *Caban.*	5. Ahau.	10. Kan.
10. Ix.	2. Ezanab.	6. Ymix.	11. Chicchan.
11. Men.	5TH MONTH.	7. Ik.	12. Cimi.
12. Cib.	3. Canac.	8. Akbal.	13. *Manik.*
13. *Caban.*	1. Ahau.	9. Kan.	1. *Lamat.*
1. *Ezanab.*	5. Ymix.	10. Chicchan.	2. Muluc.
3D MONTH.	6. Ik.	11. Cimi.	3. Oc.
2. Canac.	7. Akbal.	12. Manik.	4. Chuen.
3. Ahau.	8. Kan.	13. *Lamat.*	5. Eb.
4. Ymix.	9. Chicchan.	1. *Muluc.*	6. Been.
5. Ik.	10. Cimi.	2. Oc.	7. Ix.
6. Akbal.	11. Manik.	3. Chuen.	8. Men.
7. Kan.	12. Lamat.	4. Eb.	9. Cib.
8. Chicchan.	13. *Muluc.*	5. Been.	10. Caban.
9. Cimi.	1. *Oc.*	6. Ix.	11. Ezanab.
10. Manik.	2. Chuen.	7. Men.	10TH MONTH.
11. Lamat.	3. Eb.	8. Cib.	12. Canac.
12. Muluc.	4. Been.	9. Caban.	13. *Ahau.*
13. Oc.	5. Ix.	10. Ezanab.	1. *Ymix.*
1. *Chuen.*	6. Men.	8TH MONTH.	2. Ik.
2. Eb.	7. Cib.	11. Canac.	3. Akbal.
3. Been.	8. Caban.	12. Ahau.	4. Kan.
4. Ix.	9. Ezanab.	13. *Ymix.*	5. Chicchan.
5. Men.	6TH MONTH.	1. *Ik.*	6. Cimi.
6. Cib.	10. Canac.	2. Akbal.	7. Manik.
7. Caban.	11. Ahau.	3. Kan.	8. Lamat.
8. Ezanab.	12. Ymix.	4. Chicchan.	9. Muluc.
4TH MONTH.	13. *Ik.*	5. Cimi.	10. Oc.
9. Canac.	1. *Akbal.*	6. Manik.	11. Chuen.
10. Ahau.	2. Kan.	7. Lamat.	12. Eb.
11. Ymix.	3. Chicchan.	8. Muluc.	13. *Been.*
12. Ik.	4. Cimi.	9. Oc.	1. *Ix.*
13. *Akbal.*	5. Manik.	10. Chuen.	2. Men.
1. *Kan.*	6. Lamat.	11. Eb.	3. Cib.

4. Caban.	7. Been.	9. Lamat.	11. Akbal.
5. Ezanab.	8. Ix.	10. Muluc.	12. Kan.
11TH MONTH.	9. Men.	11. Oc.	13. *Chicchan.*
6. Cauac.	10. Cib.	12. Chuen.	1. *Cimi.*
7. Ahau.	11. Caban.	13. *Eb.*	2. Manik.
8. Ymix.	12. Ezanab.	1. *Been.*	3. Lamat.
9. Ik.	12TH MONTH.	2. Ix.	4. Muluc.
10. Akbal.	13. *Cauac.*	3. Men.	5. Oc.
11. Kan.	1. *Ahau.*	4. Cib.	6. Chuen.
12. Chicchan.	2. Imix.	5. Caban.	7. Eb.
13. *Cimi.*	3. Ik.	6. Ezanab.	8. Been.
1. *Manik.*	4. Akbal.	13TH MONTH.	9. Ix.
2. Lamat.	5. Kan.	7. Cauac.	10. Men.
3. Muluc.	6. Chicchan.	8. Ahau.	11. Cib.
4. Oc.	7. Cimi.	9. Ymix.	12. Caban.
5. Chuen.	8. Manik.	10. Ik.	13. *Ezanab.*
6. Eb.			

Now, let us follow around this outer circle comparing it with our calendar (Table I), or list of days (Table II), which, as before stated, are for the Cauac year only.

As this is a Cauac year, we must commence with the Cauac character No. 31, on the right border. Immediately to the left of this character and almost in contact with it we see a single small dot. We take for granted that this denotes 1 and that we are to begin with 1 *Cauac*. This corresponds with the first day of the first month, that is, the top number of the left-hand column of numbers in Table I or the first day in Table II. Turning to the plate we run up the line of dots to the character for *Chuen* (No. 32); immediately to the left of this we see two little bars and three dots ≡ or 13.

Turning again to our table and running down the column of the first month to the number 13 we find that it is *Chuen*, which is followed by 1 *Eb*. Turning again to the plate we observe that the character immediately above Chuen is *Eb.*, and that it has adjoining it below a single dot, or 1. Running from thence down the line of dots toward the center we reach *Ken*, immediately above which is the character for 13. Turning again to our table and starting with the 1 opposite *Eb* and running to the bottom of the column which ends with 7 and passing to 8 at the top of the second column, and running down this to 13, or following down our list of days (Table II), we find it to be *Kan*, which is followed by 1 *Chicchan*. On the plate we see the character for *Chicchan* (No. 35) immediately above that of *Kan* (No. 34), with a single small dot touching it above. Running from this upward along the row of large dots toward the outer corner we next reach the character for *Caban* (No. 36), adjoining which we see the numeral character for 13.

Running our eye down the second column of the table, from 1 opposite *Chicchan* to 13, we find it is opposite *Caban*, thus agreeing with what we find in the plate.

THE TABLEAU

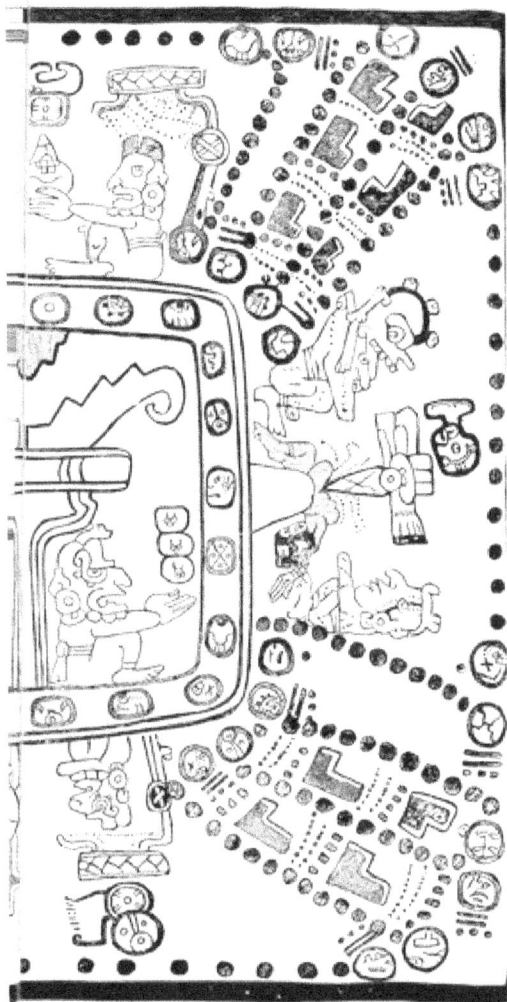

This will enable the reader to follow up the names and numbers on the table as I will now give them from *Caban* (No. 36), in the manner above shown, remembering that the movement on the plate is around the circle toward the left, that is, up the right side, toward the left on the top, down the left side, &c., and that, on the tables, after one column is completed we take the next to the right.

From *Caban* (No. 36) we go next to *Ezanab* No. 37 (the single dot is here effaced); then down the row of dots to *Oc*, No. 38, over which is the numeral for 13; then to *Chuen*, No. 39, immediately to the left (the single dot is dimly outlined immediately above it); then up the row of large dots to *Akbal* No. 40 (the numeral character for 13 is immediately to the right); then to *Kan* No. 1, immediately to the left (the single dot adjoins it on the right); then to the left along the border row of dots to *Cib* No. 2, in the upper left-hand corner, immediately under which we find the numeral character for 13.

Without following this further, I will now give a scheme or plan of the plate (Fig. 2), adding the names of the effaced characters, which the

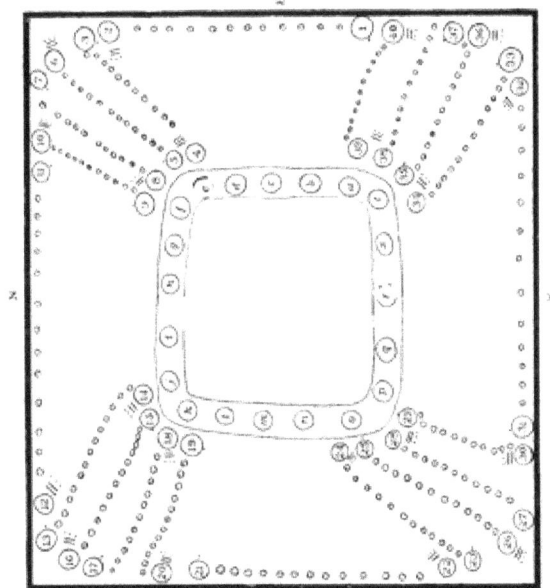

Fig. 2.—Scheme of the Tableau des Bacab.

table enables us to do by following it out in the manner explained. I
also give in Plate II another figure of the plate of the Cortesian Codex,
with the effaced characters inserted, and the interchange of *Caban* and
Eb which will be hereafter explained. This plate corresponds with the
plan or scheme shown in Fig. 2.[4]

In this we commence with Kan, numbered 1, in the top row, moving
thence toward the left as already indicated, following the course shown
by the numbers.

By this time the reader, if he has studied the plate with care, has
probably encountered one difficulty in the way of the explanation given;
that there are usually *twelve* large dots instead of *eleven*, as there should
be, between the day signs; as, for example, between Kan No. 1 and
Cib No. 2, in the upper row. This I am unable to explain, except on
the supposition that the artist included but one of the day signs in the
count, or that it was not the intention to be very exact in this respect.
The fact that the number of dots in a row is not always the same, there
being in some cases as many as thirteen, and in others but eleven,
renders the latter supposition probable. In the scheme the number of
dots in the lines is given as nearly as possible as on the plate.

As there are four different series of years in the Maya calendar, the
Cauac years, Kan years, Muluc years, and Ix years, it is necessary that
we have four different tables, similar to that given for the Cauac years,
to represent them, or to combine all in one table.

As I have adopted in my former work[5] a scheme of combining them
I will insert it here (Table III).

TABLE III.— *Condensed Maya Calendar.*

Cauac columns.	Kan columns.	Muluc columns.	Ix columns.	1 14	2 15	3 16	4 17	5 18	6	7	8	9	10	11	12	13
Cauac.	Kan.	Muluc.	Ix.	1	8	2	9	3	10	4	11	5	12	6	13	7
Ahau.	Chicchan.	Oc.	Men.	2	9	3	10	4	11	5	12	6	13	7	1	8
Ymix.	Cimi.	Chuen.	Cib.	3	10	4	11	5	12	6	13	7	1	8	2	9
Ik.	Manik.	Eb.	Caban.	4	11	5	12	6	13	7	1	8	2	9	3	10
Akbal.	Lamat.	Ben.	Ezanab.	5	12	6	13	7	1	8	2	9	3	10	4	11
Kan.	Muluc.	Ix.	Cauac.	6	13	7	1	8	2	9	3	10	4	11	5	12
Chicchan.	Oc.	Men.	Ahau.	7	1	8	2	9	3	10	4	11	5	12	6	13
Cimi.	Chuen.	Cib.	Ymix.	8	2	9	3	10	4	11	5	12	6	13	7	1
Manik.	Eb.	Caban.	Ik.	9	3	10	4	11	5	12	6	13	7	1	8	2
Lamat.	Ben.	Ezanab.	Akbal.	10	4	11	5	12	6	13	7	1	8	2	9	3
Muluc.	Ix.	Cauac.	Kan.	11	5	12	6	13	7	1	8	2	9	3	10	4
Oc.	Men.	Ahau.	Chicchan.	12	6	13	7	1	8	2	9	3	10	4	11	5
Chuen.	Cib.	Ymix.	Cimi.	13	7	1	8	2	9	3	10	4	11	5	12	6
Eb.	Caban.	Ik.	Manik.	1	8	2	9	3	10	4	11	5	12	6	13	7
Ben.	Ezanab.	Akbal.	Lamat.	2	9	3	10	4	11	5	12	6	13	7	1	8
Ix.	Cauac.	Kan.	Muluc.	3	10	4	11	5	12	6	13	7	1	8	2	9
Men.	Ahau.	Chicchan.	Oc.	4	11	5	12	6	13	7	1	8	2	9	3	10
Cib.	Ymix.	Cimi.	Chuen.	5	12	6	13	7	1	8	2	9	3	10	4	11
Caban.	Ik.	Manik.	Eb.	6	13	7	1	8	2	9	3	10	4	11	5	12
Ezanab.	Akbal.	Lamat.	Ben.	7	1	8	2	9	3	10	4	11	5	12	6	13

[4] As the reduction of the cut prevents the insertion of the names of the days, letters have been substituted for them in the quadrilateral or inner ring as follows:

In the top line.—Ymix, *a*; Chicchan, *b*; Muluc, *c*; Been, *d*, and Caban, *e*.

In the left column.—Cimi, *f*; Ik, *g*; Oc, *h*; Ix, *i*, and Ezanab, *j*.

In the bottom line.—Akbal, *k*; Manik, *l*; Chuen, *m*; Men, *n*, and Cauac, *o*.

In the right column.—Kan, *p*; Lamat, *q*; Eb, *r*; Ahau, *s*, and Cib, *t*.

[5] Study of the Manuscript Troano, p. 11.

But I must request the reader to refer to that work for an explanation of the method of using it.

By using the different columns in this table, viz, the Cauac column, the Kan column, the Muluc column, and the Ix column, in the same way as we have that of the previous Table No. I, we shall find that the plate is intended to apply in the same way to each of the four years.[1] A further correspondence will also be found in the fact that the thirteen figure columns of our table just complete the circuit of the plate, and that for the other months (or rather weeks) we commence again at the first, just as the table.

For the Kan years we commence on our scheme (Fig. 2) or the plate (No. II) at Kan No. 1, at the top, and moving around to the left, as shown, we end the thirteenth column of the calendar (13 Akbal) with Akbal No. 40. For the Muluc years we commence with Muluc No. 11, of the left side of the scheme, and end with Lamat No. 10. For the Ix years we begin with Ix No. 21, at the bottom, and end with Been No. 20. For the Cauac years we begin with Cauac No. 31, at the right side, and end with Ezanab No. 30.

By following this plan we will find that the characters and numerals in the plate agree in every case with the names and numbers of the days in the table, showing that I have properly interpreted this part of the plate. It is impossible that there should be such exact agreement if I were wrong in my interpretation.

This, it seems to me, will show beyond controversy the respective quarters to which the different years are assigned in the plate—Kan to the top, where this year begins; Muluc to the left; Ix to the bottom, and Cauac to the right hand; and, as a consequence, that the top is the east; left, north; bottom, west, and right hand, south. But this is a point to be discussed hereafter.

Our next step is to ascertain the object in view in placing the twenty day characters around the inner space in the order we find them. Here I confess we shall encounter greater difficulty in arriving at a satisfactory explanation; still, I think we shall be able to show one object in view in this singular arrangement, although we fall short of a complete interpretation.

If we commence with Ymix, in the upper line of the quadrilateral, and move around it to the left, as heretofore, noting the days in each side in the order they come on the plate, we find them to be as follows:

In the top line: Ymix, Chicchan, Muluc, Been, Eb.

Left column: Cimi, Ik, Oc, Ix, Ezanab.

Bottom line: Akbal, Manik, Chuen, Men, Cauac.

Right column (upward): Kan, Lamat, Caban, Ahau, Cib.

Now let us take the twenty days, in the order they stand in the cal-

[1] It is worthy of note that the numerals on the plate apply only to the years 1 Cauac, 1 Kan, 1 Muluc, and 1 Ix, the first years of an Indication or week of years.

endar, commencing with Kan, writing them in four columns, placing
one name in each in succession, thus:

Kan.	Chicchan.	Cimi.	Manik.
Lamat.	Muluc.	Oc.	Chuen.
Eb.	Been.	Ix.	Men.
Cib.	Caban.	Ezanab.	Caune.
Ahau.	Ymix.	Ik.	Akbal.

If we commence with any other day the groups will contain respectively the same days, as, for example, if we begin with Ymix as here
shown (Table IV).

As I am inclined to believe the author of the plate adopted this order
I shall use and refer to this table in speaking of these groups.

TABLE IV.

1.	2.	3.	4.
Ymix.	Ik.	Akbal.	Kan.
Chicchan.	Cimi.	Manik.	Lamat.
Muluc.	Oc.	Chuen.	Eb.
Been.	Ix.	Men.	Cib.
Caban.	Ezanab.	Caune.	Ahau.

Examining the five names in the third column we find they are the
same as those in the bottom line of the quadrilateral of the plate, and
also in the same order. Those of the second column are the same as
those in the left column of the plate, though not precisely in the same
order; those in the first column the same as those in the top line of the
plate, except that in our column we have Caban in place of Eb; and
those in the fourth column the same as those in the right column of the
plate, except that in our column we have Eb instead of Caban. I am
satisfied, therefore, that the artist who made the plate has transposed
the characters Eb and Caban; that in place of Eb, the left-hand character of the upper line, there should be Caban, and in place of Caban,
the middle character of the right column, there should be Eb, and have
made this change in my scheme (Fig. 2) and in Plate II.

This, I admit, has the appearance of making an arbitrary change to
suit a theory; but besides the strong evidence in favor of this change
shown by the arrangement of the days in four columns just given, I
propose to present other testimony.

That the characters here interpreted *Eb* and *Caban* are the same as
those given by Landa, and in the Manuscript Troano we have positive
evidence in the tortous line in the outer space, of which we have already
given an explanation. Hence there is no escape from the difficulty by
supposing the artist had reversed the characters in their reference to
the names. Either he has reversed them as to place, or we are mis-
taken in our supposition as to how the four groups were obtained.

If we turn, now, to the Manuscript Troano, and examine the day columns, comparing them with these four groups as I have corrected them
by this single transposition, I think we shall find one clue at least to the
object of the arrangement we observe on this plate. As but few are
likely to have the Manuscript at hand, I will refer to Chapter VII of my
work (*A Study of the Manuscript Troano*), where a large number of these
day columns are given. In making the comparison I ask the reader to
use my scheme (Fig. 2). Commencing with the first column on page
165, we find it to be Manik, Canac, Chuen, Akbal, Men, precisely the
same days as in the bottom line. The next two on the same page are
first Akbal, Muluc, Men, Ymix, Manik, and second, Ben, Canac, Chicchan, Chuen, Caban, taken alternately from the bottom and top lines
of the quadrilateral.

On the lower part of the same page (165) is another column with the
following days, Ahau, Oc, Eb, Ik, Kan, Ix, Cib, Cimi, Lamat, taken alternately from the right and left sides of the plate as given in our scheme.
But there are only nine names in the column, when the order in which
they are taken would seem to require ten. By examining the plate (IV)
in the Manuscript the reader will see that there are indications that one
at the top has been obliterated. By examining the right and left columns of our scheme we see that the omitted one is Ezanab. By counting
the intervals between the days, as explained in my work, we find them
to be alternately two and ten, and that by this rule the missing day
is Ezanab. The reader will notice in these examples that Eb and Caban
belong to the positions I have given them in my scheme (Fig. 2).

Turning to page 166 we find the first column (from "second division,"
Plate IV) to be Kan, Cib, Lamat, Ahau, Eb, the same days as in the
right column of our scheme. The second column, Canac, Chuen, Akbal,
Men, Manik, the same as the lower line of the scheme. The first column
on page 167 has the same days as the right column of the plate, as corrected in my scheme and our Plate II. The second column of this page
presents a new combination. We have so far found the names of a day
column all in a single group or line of our plate, or taken alternately
from opposite sides; here we find them taken alternately from each of
the four sides of the quadrilateral moving around to the left in the order
I have heretofore explained. The days in this column are Caban, Ik,
Manik, Eb, Caban. One is taken from the upper line (as corrected),
then one from the left side, next from the bottom line, then from the
right side (as corrected), and then the same from the top line.

It is unnecessary for me to give more examples, as the reader can
make the comparison for himself; and he will, as I believe, find my
theory sustained.

The only real objection I can see to my explanation of the arrangement of the days in this circle is the fact that it necessitates the transposition of two characters, but it is not unreasonable to suppose that
the artist may have made this one mistake.

    3 ETH——2

Fortunately we find on Plates 18 and 19 of the Codex Peresianus[1] what appears to be a complete confirmation of the theory here advanced.

This is a kind of tabular arrangement of certain days, with accompanying numbers, as shown in our Fig. 3, which is an exact copy of those portions of Plates 18 and 19 of the Codex Peresianus, to which I refer.

I also give in Table V the names of the days and the numbers corresponding with the symbols and characters of Fig. 3. In this table the erased days and obliterated numerals are restored, these being in italics to distinguish them from those on the plate.

TABLE V.

10.	*Kan.*	8.	Cib.	6.	Lamat.	4.	Ahau.	2.	Eb.
10.	*Lamat.*	8.	Ahau.	6.	Eb.	4.	Kan.	2.	Cib.
10.	*Eb.*	8.	Kan.	6.	Cib.	4.	Lamat.	2.	Ahau.
10.	*Cib.*	8.	Lamat.	6.	Ahau.	4.	Eb.	2.	Kan.
10.	*Ahau.*	8.	Eb.	6.	Kan.	4.	Cib.	2.	Lamat.
13.	*Kan.*	*11.*	*Cib.*	9.	Lamat.	7.	Ahau.	5.	Eb.
13.	*Lamat.*	*11.*	*Ahau.*	9.	Eb.	7.	Kan.	5.	Cib.
13.	*Eb.*	*11.*	*Kan.*	9.	Cib.	7.	Lamat.	5.	Ahau.
13.	*Cib.*	*11.*	*Lamat.*	9.	Ahau.	7.	Eb.	5.	Kan.
13.	*Ahau.*	*11.*	*Eb.*	9.	Kan.	7.	Cib.	5.	Lamat.
3.	Kan.	1.	*Cib.*	*12.*	*Lamat.*				
3.	Lamat.	1.	*Ahau.*	*12.*	*Eb.*				
3.	Eb.	1.	*Kan.*	*12.*	*Cib.*				
3.	Cib.	1.	*Lamat.*	*12.*	*Ahau.*				
3.	Ahau.	1.	*Eb.*	*12.*	*Kan.*				

An inspection of this table shows us that the five days repeated in each column are the same as those on the right of the quadrilateral of our scheme (Fig. 2), and are exactly in the order obtained by arranging the days of the month in four columns in the manner heretofore shown. (See column 4, Table IV.)

If I am correct in my supposition, we then have one clue to, if not a full explanation of, the method of obtaining the day columns in the Manuscript Troano.

---

[1] *Manuscrit dit Mexicain No. 2.*—The Bureau of Ethnology has had the good fortune to obtain a copy of Duruy's photographic reproduction of this Manuscript, of which, according to Leclerc (Bibliotheca Americana), only ten copies were issued, though Brasseur in his Bibliothèque Mexico-Guatémalienne (p. 95) affirms that the edition consisted of fifty copies. The full title is as follows: "*Manuscrit dit Mexicain No. 2 de la Bibliothèque Impériale Photographié (sans réduction). Par ordre de S. E. M. Duruy, Ministre de l'Instruction publique, Président de la Commission scientifique du Mexique.* Paris, 1864."

Rosny has given a fac-simile copy from the two plates here referred to in Plate XVI of his *Essai sur le Déchiffrement de l'Écriture Hieratique.*

Not this only, for this table of the Codex Peresianus furnishes us also the explanation of the red numerals found over the day columns in the Manuscript Troano. Take, for example, Plate XIX, first or upper division, given also in my Study of The Manuscript Troano, p. 176, here the number is IV, corresponding with column 4 of the above table (V), where the days are the same and the numeral prefixed to each day is 4. Plate XXVI (Study Manuscript Troano, p. 177), lower division, the days are the same and the number over the column is XIII, corresponding with the sixth column of Table V. This corroborates the opinion I expressed in my former work, that the number over the column was to be applied to each day of the column.

Why is the order of the numerals in the extract from the Codex Peresianus precisely the same as the numbering of the Ahaues? I answer, because each column, if taken as referring to the four classes of years, will, when the number of the month is given, determine just the years of an Ahau; or a fancy of the artist to follow an order considered sacred.

To illustrate, let us take the next to the right-hand column of the table where the numeral is 1, and let us assume the month to be Pop, or the 1st. Then we have 1 Cib, 1 Ahau, 1 Kan, 1 Lamat, and 1 Eb of the first month, and from this data we are to find the years. As there can be four years found to each of these days, that is a Cauac year with 1 Cib in the first month, a Muluc year with one Cib in the first month, a Kan year with one Cib in the first month, an Ix year with one Cib in the first month, a Kan year with one Ahau in the first month, &c., it is evident that there will be, as the total result, just twenty years.

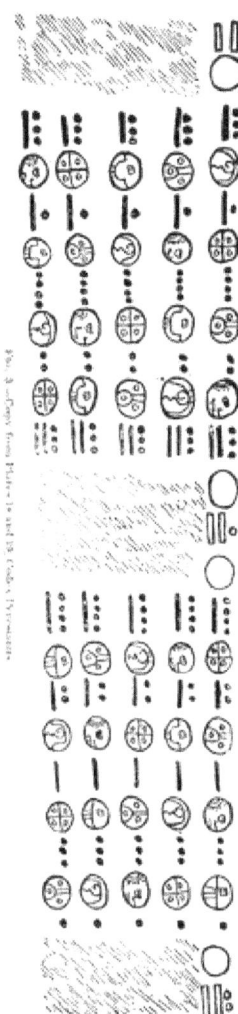

Fig. 3.—Copy from Plate 18 of the Codex Peresianus.

As I cannot repeat here, without occupying too much space, the method of finding the years, I must refer the reader to Study Manuscript Troano, p. 23, *et al.* Hunting them out, by using our Table III, we find them to be as follows:

	1 Cib.	1 *Ahau.*	1. *Kan.*	1. *Lamat.*	1 *Eb.*
Years	10 Cauac.	13 Cauac.	9 Cauac.	5 Cauac.	1 Cauac.
Years	2 Kan.	11 Kan.	1 Kan.	10 Kan.	6 Kan.
Years	7 Muluc.	3 Muluc.	12 Muluc.	8 Muluc.	11 Muluc.
Years	12 Ix.	8 Ix.	4 Ix.	13 Ix.	9 Ix.

If we turn now to Table XVII (Study Manuscript Troano p. 44), we will find that these are precisely the counted years (those in the space inclosed by the dotted lines) in Ahau number VI.

If we assume the month to be the 11th then the numbers of the Ahaues will correspond exactly with the numbers of the columns of our Table V.[*]

As it may be supposed that using the same numeral to any five days of the twenty in this way will produce a similar result, let us test it by an example. For this purpose we select the same column of our foregoing table, No. V—that with the number 1 prefixed—Cib, Ahau, Kan, Lamat, Eb, but in place of Lamat we insert Cimi. Hunting out the years as heretofore we find them to be as follows:

	1 Cib.	1 *Ahau.*	1 *Kan.*	1 *Cimi.*	1 *Eb.*
Years	10 Cauac.	13 Cauac	9 Cauac.	7 Cauac.	1 Cauac.
Years	2 Kau	11 Kan.	1 Kan.	12 Kan.	6 Kan.
Years	7 Muluc.	3 Muluc.	12 Muluc.	10 Muluc.	11 Muluc.
Years	12 Ix.	8 Ix.	4 Ix.	2 Ix.	9 Ix.

If we try to locate these years in an Ahau in Table XVII (Study Manuscript Troano p. 44), we shall find it impossible to do so, nor can we locate them in any table that can be made which has either twenty-four or twenty years in an Ahau, while on the other hand the twenty years obtained by using a column of the table from the Codex Peresianus can be located in some one of the Ahaues obtained by any division of the Grand Cycle into consecutive groups of twenty-four years that can be made. It would require too much space to prove this assertion, but any one who doubts its correctness can test it.

As the extract we have given from the Codex Peresianus relates only to one of the four groups of days—that on the right of the quadrilateral—I will supply in the following tables, Nos. VII, VIII, and IX. the arrangement of the groups of the other three sides; adding the other (Table VI), also, so as to bring the four together in the order of the sides of the quadrilateral, commencing with the line on the right, next the upper one, and so on.

While this is undoubtedly the order in which they are to be taken; which is the proper one to commence with? is a question yet to be discussed.

---

[*]An illustration can be seen on pp. 36-40, Study Manuscript Troano.

TABLE VI.

10. Kan.	8. Cib.	6. Lamat.	4. Ahau.	2. Eb.
10. Lamat.	8. Ahau.	6. Eb.	4. Kan.	2. Cib.
10. Eb.	8. Kan.	6. Cib.	4. Lamat.	2. Ahau.
10. Cib.	8. Lamat.	6. Ahau.	4. Eb.	2. Kan.
10. Ahau.	8. Eb.	6. Kan.	4. Cib.	2. Lamat.
13. Kan.	11. Cib.	9. Lamat.	7. Ahau.	5. Eb.
13. Lamat.	11. Ahau.	9. Eb.	7. Kan.	5. Cib.
13. Eb.	11. Kan.	9. Cib.	7. Lamat.	5. Ahau.
13. Cib.	11. Lamat.	9. Ahau.	7. Eb.	5. Kan.
13. Ahau.	11. Eb.	9. Kan.	7. Cib.	5. Lamat.
3. Kan.	1. Cib.	12. Lamat.		
3. Lamat.	1. Ahau.	12. Eb.		
3. Eb.	1. Kan.	12. Cib.		
3. Cib.	1. Lamat.	12. Ahau.		
3. Ahau.	1. Eb.	12. Kan.		

TABLE VII.

10. Ymix.	8. Been.	6. Chicchan.	4. Caban.	2. Muluc.
10. Chicchan.	8. Caban.	6. Muluc.	4. Ymix.	2. Been.
10. Muluc.	8. Ymix.	6. Been.	4. Chicchan.	2. Caban.
10. Been.	8. Chicchan.	6. Caban.	4. Muluc.	2. Ymix
10. Caban.	8. Muluc.	6. Ymix.	4. Been.	2. Chicchan.
13. Ymix.	11. Been.	9. Chicchan.	7. Caban.	5. Muluc.
13. Chicchan.	11. Caban.	9. Muluc.	7. Ymix.	5. Been.
13. Muluc.	11. Ymix.	9. Been.	7. Chicchan.	5. Caban.
13. Been.	11. Chicchan.	9. Caban.	7. Muluc.	5. Ymix.
13. Caban.	11. Muluc.	9. Ymix.	7. Been.	5. Chicchan.
3. Ymix.	1. Been.	12. Chicchan		
3. Chicchan.	1. Caban.	12. Muluc.		
3. Muluc.	1. Ymix.	12. Been.		
3. Been.	1. Chicchan.	12. Caban.		
3. Caban.	1. Muluc.	12. Ymix.		

TABLE VIII.

10. Oc.	8. Ik.	6. Ix.	4. Cimi.	2. Ezanab.
10. Ix.	8. Cimi.	6. Ezanab.	4. Oc.	2. Ik.
10. Ezanab.	8. Oc.	6. Ik.	4. Ix.	2. Cimi.
10. Ik.	8. Ix.	6. Cimi.	4. Ezanab.	2. Oc.
10. Cimi.	8. Ezanab.	6. Oc.	4. Ik.	2. Ix.

13. i e.	11. Ik.	9. Ix.	7. Cimi.	5. Ezanab.
13. Ix.	11. Cimi.	9. Ezanab.	7. Oc.	5. Ik.
13. Ezanab.	11. Oc.	9. Ik.	7. Ix.	5. Cimi.
13. Ik.	11. Ix.	9. Cimi.	7. Ezanab.	5. Oc.
13. Cimi.	11. Ezanab.	9. Oc.	7. Ik.	5. Ix.
3. Oc.	1. Ik.	12. Ix.		
3. Ix.	1. Cimi.	12. Ezanab.		
3. Ezanab.	1. Oc.	12. Ik.		
3. Ik.	1. Ix.	12. Cimi.		
3. Cimi.	1. Ezanab.	12. Oc.		

TABLE IX.

10. Men.	8. Manik.	6. Canac.	4. Chuen.	2. Akbal.
10. Cauac.	8. Chuen.	6. Akbal.	4. Men.	2. Manik.
10. Akbal.	8. Men.	6. Manik.	4. Cauac.	2. Chuen.
10. Manik.	8. Cauac.	6. Chuen.	4. Akbal.	2. Men.
10. Chuen.	8. Akbal.	6. Men.	4. Manik.	2. Cauac.
13. Men.	11. Manik.	9. Cauac.	7. Chuen.	5. Akbal.
13. Cauac.	11. Chuen.	9. Akbal.	7. Men.	5. Manik.
13. Akbal.	11. Men.	9. Manik.	7. Cauac.	5. Chuen.
13. Manik.	11. Cauac.	9. Chuen.	7. Akbal.	5. Men.
13. Chuen.	11. Akbal.	9. Men.	7. Manik.	5. Cauac.
3. Men.	1. Manik.	12. Cauac.		
3. Cauac.	1. Chuen.	12. Akbal.		
3. Akbal.	1. Men.	12. Manik.		
3. Manik.	1. Cauac.	12. Chuen.		
3. Chuen.	1. Akbal.	12. Men.		

There is still another and somewhat probable supposition in regard to the object of this division of the days of the month into groups of five, which will obviate one objection to the explanation given in my former work, viz, the very large number of dates given in the Manuscript Troano on the supposition that there are four years to each numeral connected with the day columns. It is possible that the days of one group indicate the year intended; that is, whether it is a Cauac, Kan, Mulac, or Ix year.

For example, column No. 4 (Table IV), or some other one of the four, may relate to Kan years; No. 1 to Mulac years; No. 2 to Ix years, and No. 3 to Cauac years. Assuming this to be correct, then the example heretofore given, where the days named are 1 Cib, 1 Ahau, 1 Kan, 1 Lamat, and 1 Eb, and the month the first (Pop), would indicate only the years 7 Mulac, 3 Mulac, 12 Mulac, 8 Mulac, and 11 Mulac. These would all come in Ahau No. VI, as before, but would indicate that the festival, or whatever they referred to, occurred but once every four years,

in the first month of the year. Hence if the five days of a column (as
of the Manuscript Troano) are all taken from one side of the quadrilateral of our scheme they will refer to years of one dominical sign only; if
alternately from opposite sides, then to the years of two dominical signs,
but if taken alternately from the four sides they would refer to the four
classes of years. This will reduce the number of dates in the Manuscript Troano very considerably from the other supposition, but will not
in any way change the position of the Ahaues in the Grand Cycle.

As one further item of evidence in regard to this method of arranging
the twenty days of the month in four groups or columns, I call attention
to what is found on Plate 32 of the Dresden Codex. Here we find the
four columns of five days each, corresponding precisely with the arrangement of the Maya days into four groups, as heretofore. I present
here the arrangement as found on this plate:

TABLE X.

a.	b.	c.	d.
Manik.	Cib.	Chicchan.	Ix.
Chuen.	Ahau.	Mulue.	Ezanab.
Men.	Kan.	Been.	Ik.
Camac.	Lamat.	Caban.	Cimi.
Akbal.	Eb.	Ymix.	Oc.

It will be seen by comparing this grouping with that in Table IV
that column a of this plate contains the same days as column 3 of the
table; column b the same as column 4; column c the same as column 1,
and column d the same as column 2.

But so far I have found no entirely satisfactory explanation of the
order given in many of these columns and in three of the sides of the
quadrilateral of the Cortesian plate.

As this discussion is preliminary to a discussion of the assignment of
the symbols of the cardinal points, it becomes necessary, in order to
bring in all the evidence bearing upon the question, to examine certain
points of the Mexican calendar system, as given by various authors and
as exhibited in the Mexican Codices.

If we refer now to Plate 43 of the Borgian Codex, as found in Kingsborough's "Mexican Antiquities," Vol. III, a photo-engraved copy of
which is presented in our Fig. 4, we shall, as I believe, not only find additional confirmation of the views I have advanced in reference to the
peculiar arrangement of the days around the quadrilateral in the plate
of the Cortesian Codex, but also strong evidence of a common origin of
the Mexican and Central American calendars.

This plate of the Borgian Codex, which is Mexican and not Maya,
consists of four groups, the whole arranged in the form of a square; each
group, also a square, is surrounded by a serpent, the heads of the four
serpents being brought near together at the center, which is indicated

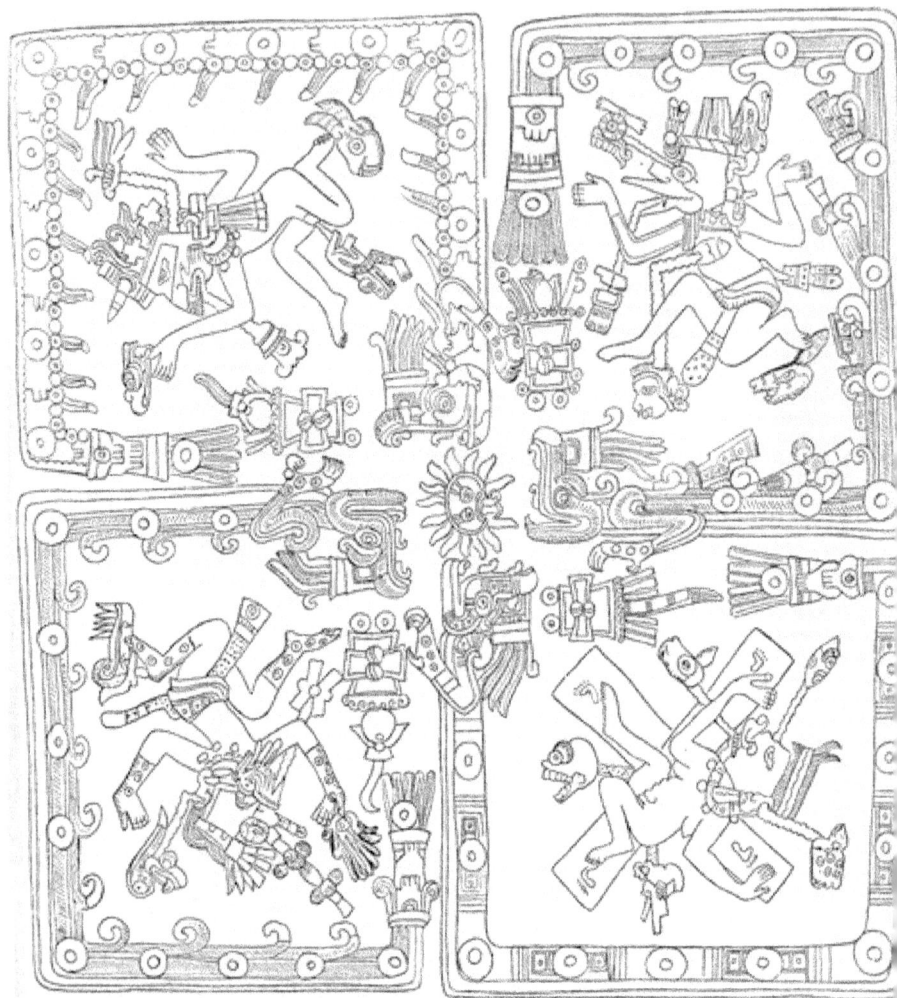

Fig. 4.—Copy of plate 43. Borgian Codex.

by the figure of the sun. Each of these serpents, as I have heretofore intimated,[9] probably denotes one of the four year series of the
cycle of fifty-two years, just as in the Maya cycle we would say "the
Canac series," "Kan series," etc.[10] The thirteen years of each series
is denoted by the small circles on the serpents. The four large figures
are, as we shall hereafter see, fanciful representations of certain ideas
held by this people in regard to the four cardinal points, each probably
with its significant color as understood by the artist, and each probably
indicating one of the four year bearers.

But at present our attention is directed to something else to be found
on this plate. In each of the four spaces and around each of the large
figures we observe five Mexican day symbols connected usually with the
main figure by heavy waved colored lines. What is the signification
of these day symbols in this connection? Precisely the same, I believe,
as those in the four sides of the quadrilateral in the Codex Cortesianus.
But first I would remark that the waved, colored, connecting lines have
no other signification than to denote the parts of the body to which the
days are here severally assigned; hence, as they have no bearing on the
questions now under discussion, I shall have no occasion to take any
further notice of them.

If we arrange the Mexican days in four columns as we did the Maya,
that is, placing the first name in the first column, the second in the second column, and so on, following the usual orthography and the order
given, the groups will be as follows:

TABLE XI.

1.	2.	3.	4.
Cipactli.	Ehecatl.	Calli.	Cuetzpalin.
Coatl.	Miquiztli.	Mazatl.	Tochtli.
Atl.	Itzquintli.	Ozomatli.	Malinalli.
Acatl.	Oceloti.	Quauhtli.	Cozcaquauhtli.
Ollin.	Tecpatl.	Quiahuitl.	Xochitl.

Or, to give them their English equivalents as we usually find them, as
follows:

TABLE XII.

1.	2.	3.	4.
Dragon.	Wind.	House.	Lizard.
Snake.	Death.	Deer.	Rabbit.
Water.	Dog.	Monkey.	Grass.
Cane.	Tiger.	Eagle.	Vulture.
Movement.	Flint.	Rain.	Flower.

---

[9] Study Manuscript Troano, p. 86.

[10] Possibly each serpent represents one indication of thirteen years, but the proper
answer to this question is not important in the present investigation.

Comparing these columns with the symbols around each one of these large figures we find that to each one of the latter are assigned the days of one of these four columns. In the lower left-hand square, to the large green figure, those in column 1; thus, at the left foot, the Dragon; to the back of the head, the Snake; to the eye, Cane; in the right hand, Water; and below the elbow, but connected with the mouth, Ollin or movement (sometimes translated earthquake). To the yellow figure, in the lower right-hand square, are applied those of the second column; to the black figure, in the upper right-hand square, those of the third column; and to the red figure, in the upper left-hand square, those of the fourth column. There is therefore scarcely any doubt that this arrangement is for precisely the same purpose as that in the plate of the Codex Cortesianus.

As proof that the Mexicans used these combinations in much the same way as the Maya priests I call attention to the following examples:

On Plate 59, of the same (Borgian) Codex, we find two columns of days, one on the right and the other on the left, as follows: .

Left column.	Right column.
Tochtli.	Quauhtli.
Ehecatl.	Atl.
Cozcaquauhtli.	Calli.
Itzquintli.	Ollin.
Cuetzpalin.	Ozomatli.
Tecpatl.	Coatl.
Malinalli.	Quiahuitl.
Miquiztli.	Acatl.
Xochitl.	Mazatl.
Ocelotl.	Cipactli.

Comparing these with the names in the four columns (Table XI), we find that those on the left were taken alternately from columns 4 and 2, and those on the right alternately from columns 3 and 1. On Plates 61 and 62 we find substantially the same arrangement, or at least the same idea as the extract from Codex Peresianus, heretofore referred to. On these two plates (embracing all of 61, and the lower left-hand square of 62) we find five squares, each one bordered on two sides with the symbol of a single day repeated thirteen times and accompanied by numeral signs.

Commencing with the square on page 62, where the repeated day symbol is Cipactli, and reading the line from left to right and up the column, we find the numbers to be as follows, filling out the effaced ones in the line:

Cipactli, 1, 8, 2, 9, 3, 10, 4, 11, 5, 12, 6, 13, 7 (the symbol being repeated with each number.)

In the next, the lower right-hand square on Plate 61, where the day is Coatl, the numbers, reading the same way, are as follows (filling out one effaced one):

Coatl, 5, 12, 6, 13, 7, 1, 8, 2, 9, 3, 10, 4, 11.

Taking the lower left-hand square next, the day *Atl,* and reading in the same direction, we find the numbers to be as follows (filling out two effaced groups):

Atl, 9, 3, 10, 4, 11, 5, 12, 6, 13, 7, 1, 8, 2.

We take the upper left-hand next, reading from left to right and up:

Acatl, 13, 7, 1, 8, 2, 9, 3, 10, 4, 11, 5, 12, 6.

Lastly, the upper right-hand square, reading the same way as the last.

Ollin, 4, 11, 5, 12, 6, 13, 7, 1, 8, 2, 9, 3, 10.

We have only to turn to our abridged calendar (Table III) to find this explained. If we take the Ix column and select every fourth day, to wit, Ix, Ezanab, Ik, Cimi, and Oc, and read the line of numbers opposite each, we shall find them corresponding precisely with those mentioned here. For instance, those opposite *Ix* the same as those opposite *Cipactli,* &c.

We further notice that these five names, *Cipactli, Coatl, Atl, Acatl,* and *Ollin,* or, to use the English names, Dragon, Snake, Water, Cane, and Movement, are precisely those of column 1 of the arrangement of the Mexican days as heretofore given (Table XI).

On plates 13-17 of the Vatican Codex, B, Kingsborough, Vol. III, we find precisely the same arrangement as that just described, and where the numerals are so distinct that there can be no doubt in regard to any of them. The days are exactly the same—Cipactli, Coatl, Atl, Acatl, and Ollin—and in the same order, but the plates are to be taken in the reverse order, commencing with 17, and the columns and lines are to be read

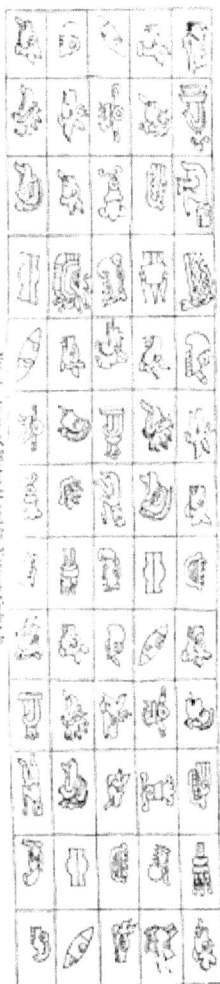

thus: Commencing at the bottom at the right hand, upward to the top, and then along the line toward the left.

On Plate 58 of the Borgian Codex we find six lines of days with five in each line. Five out of these six lines are composed of the five days just named, simply varied as to the respective positions they occupy in the line, but maintaining the same order.

On Plate 17, same Codex, we see two lines corresponding with the first and second columns of the arrangement of the days heretofore given.

But without further reference to these smaller or isolated groups, we have conclusive proof of this method of arranging the days among the Mexicans, in three extended series—one found on Plates 49–56 of the Vatican Codex B; one on Plates 31–38 of the Borgian Codex, and another on Plates 1–8 of the Bologna Codex.

I give here the arrangement found in the first, which is precisely the same as that of the Borgian Codex, except that this is to be read from the left to the right, and that of the Borgian Codex from the right to the left, both commencing with the bottom line (numbered 5 in the following list):

A photo-engraved copy of one plate of the former is also given in Fig. 5, as it furnishes proof that the days and the order in which they follow each other are the same as I have given them.

For the benefit of English readers the list is given in the English equivalents of the Mexican names.[13]

TABLE XIII.

1. Water.	Dog.	Monkey.	Grass.	Cane.
2. Movement.	Flint.	Rain.	Flower.	Dragon.
3. Snake.	Death.	Deer.	Rabbit.	Water.
4. Cane.	Tiger.[14]	Eagle.	Vulture.	Movement.
5. Dragon.	Wind.	House.	Lizard.	Snake.
1. Tiger.	Eagle.	Vulture.	Movement.	Flint.
2. Wind.	House.	Lizard.	Snake.	Death.
3. Dog.	Monkey.	Grass.	Cane.	Tiger.
4. Flint.	Rain.	Flower.	Dragon.	Wind.
5 Death.	Deer.	Rabbit.	Water.	Dog.
1. Rain.	Flower.	Dragon.	Wind.	House.
2. Deer.	Rabbit.	Water.	Dog.	Monkey.
3. Eagle.	Vulture.	Movement.	Flint.	Rain.
4. House.	Lizard.	Snake.	Death.	Deer.
5. Monkey.	Grass.	Cane.	Tiger.	Eagle.

[13] In order to accommodate the list to the paging it is divided into sections, the second section to follow to the right of the first; the third to the right of the second, and so on to the last, as though extended continuously to the right. Those numbered 1 would then form one continuous transverse line, as would also those numbered 2, 3, 4 and 5 respectively.

[14] In the original, *Deer*, certainly an error.

1. Lizard.	Snake.	Death.	Deer.	Rabbit.
2. Grass.	Cane.	Tiger.	Eagle.	Vulture.
3. Flower.	Dragon.	Wind.	House.	Lizard.
4. Rabbit.	Water.	Dog.	Monkey.	Grass.
5. Vulture.	Movement.	Flint.	Rain.	Flower.
1. Water.	Dog.	Monkey.	Grass.	Cane.
2. Movement.	Flint.	Rain.	Flower.	Dragon.
3. Snake.	Death.	Deer.	Rabbit.	Water.
4. Cane.	Tiger.	Eagle.	Vulture.	Movement.
5. Dragon.	Wind.	House.	Lizard.	Snake.
1. Tiger.	Eagle.	Vulture.	Movement.	Flint.
2. Wind.	House.	Lizard.	Snake.	Death.
3. Dog.	Monkey.	Grass.	Cane.	Tiger.
4. Flint.	Rain.	Flower.	Dragon.	Wind.
5. Death.	Deer.	Rabbit.	Water.	Dog.
1. Rain.	Flower.	Dragon.	Wind.	House.
2. Deer.	Rabbit.	Water.	Dog.	Monkey.
3. Eagle.	Vulture.	Movement.	Flint.	Rain.
4. House.	Lizard.	Snake.	Death.	Deer.
5. Monkey.	Grass.	Cane.	Tiger.	Eagle.
1. Lizard.	Snake.	Death.	Deer.	Rabbit.
2. Grass.	Cane.	Tiger.	Eagle.	Vulture.
3. Flower.	Dragon.	Wind.	House.	Lizard.
4. Rabbit.	Water.	Dog.	Monkey.	Grass.
5. Vulture.	Movement.	Flint.	Rain.	Flower.
1. Water.	Dog.	Monkey.	Grass.	Cane.
2. Movement.	Flint.	Rain.	Flower.	Dragon.
3. Snake.	Death.	Deer.	Rabbit.	Water.
4. Cane.	Tiger.	Eagle.	Vulture.	Movement.
5. Dragon.	Wind.	House.	Lizard.	Snake.
1. Tiger.[1]	Eagle.	Vulture.	Movement.	Flint.
2. Wind.	House.	Lizard.	Snake.	Death.
3. Dog.	Monkey.	Grass.	Cane.	Tiger.
4. Flint.	Rain.	Flower.	Dragon.	Wind.
5. Death.	Deer.	Rabbit.	Water.	Dog.
1. Rain.	Flower.			
2. Deer.	Rabbit.			
3. Eagle.	Vulture.			
4. House.	Lizard.			
5. Monkey.	Grass.			

[1] In the original, *Deer.*

If we examine the columns of this list, we see that each one contains the days of some one of the four columns of the arrangement heretofore given; not always in precisely the same order, but the same days.

Without stopping to attempt a further explanation of this calendar or *Tonalamatl*, which is not within the scope of our present purpose, I merely remark that it is evidently a representation of the Mexican "cycle of two hundred and sixty days," or thirteen months, the common multiple of 4, 5, 13, and 20, and hence a cycle, at the completion of which the day, numeral, &c. (except the month), will be the same as at the beginning.

PLATE 44 OF THE FEJERVARY CODEX,

As a connecting link between the particular topic now under discussion and the consideration of the symbols of the cardinal points, I wish to refer to one plate of the Fejervary Codex, to wit, Plate 44, *a facsimile* of which is presented in Plate III:

A little careful inspection of this plate will suffice to convince the reader that it was gotten up upon the same plan and for the same purpose as the "Tableau des Bacab," or plate copied from the Codex Cortesianus, which is reproduced in our Plate I.

The sacred tree or cross, which is represented but once in that plate, and that in the central area, is here shown four times—once in each of the four outer spaces opposite the four sides of the inner area.

It is true we do not find here the intermediate ring (or quadrilateral) of days, but these are not wanting, for the four groups, corresponding with those on the four sides of the quadrilateral, are here found at the four corners wedged in between the colored loops, one group of five at each corner. The chief marked resemblance is to be found in the outer looped line, in which the day characters are connected by rows of dots. But here the lines and loops, although almost precisely in the form and relation to each other as in the plate of the Cortesian Codex, are variously and brightly colored, and the rows of dots are inclosed by lateral lines.

Now for the proof that it is designed for the same purpose as the looped line on the other plate. But it is necessary that I present first, in a tabular form, a Mexican calendar (Table XIV) similar to the condensed Maya calendar heretofore given.

I also give, immediately following, a list of Mexican days for thirteen months, the number necessary to make the circuit of the plate, just as the list of Maya days heretofore given. In this case I have used the English equivalents of the Mexican words for the benefit of English readers.

31

TABLE XIV.—Condensed Mexican calendar.

Tochtli years.	Acatl years.	Tecpatl years.	Calli years.	Numbers of the months.												
				1	2	3	4	5	6	7	8	9	10	11	12	13
				14	15	16	17	18								
Coacaquauh-tli.	Cipactli	Miquiztli ...	Oeomatli....	1	8	2	9	3	10	4	11	5	12	6	13	7
Ollin.........	Ehecatl ...	Mazatl	Malinalli....	2	9	3	10	4	11	5	12	6	13	7	1	8
Tecpatl	Calli	Tochtli	Acatl	3	10	4	11	5	12	6	13	7	1	8	2	9
Quiahuitl	Cuetzpalin..	Atl	Ocelotl	4	11	5	12	6	13	7	1	8	2	9	3	10
Xochitl	Coatl	Itzcuintli.....	Quauhtli	5	12	6	13	7	1	8	2	9	3	10	4	11
Cipactli	Miquiztli ...	Ozomatli ...	Coacaquauh-tli.	6	13	7	1	8	2	9	3	10	4	11	5	12
Ehecatl	Mazatl	Malinalli ...	Ollin.........	7	1	8	2	9	3	10	4	11	5	12	6	13
Calli	Tochtli	Acatl......	Tecpatl	8	2	9	3	10	4	11	5	12	6	13	7	1
Cuetzpalin...	Atl	Ocelotl......	Quiahuitl	9	3	10	4	11	5	12	6	13	7	1	8	2
Coatl	Itzcuintli....	Quauhtli ...	Xochitl	10	4	11	5	12	6	13	7	1	8	2	9	3
Miquiztli ...	Ozomatli ...	Coacaquauh-tli.	Cipactli	11	5	12	6	13	7	1	8	2	9	3	10	4
Mazatl	Malinalli ...	Ollin	Ehecatl......	12	6	13	7	1	8	2	9	3	10	4	11	5
Tochtli	Acatl	Tecpatl	Calli	13	7	1	8	2	9	3	10	4	11	5	12	6
Atl	Ocelotl......	Quiahuitl....	Cuetzpalin...	1	8	2	9	3	10	4	11	5	12	6	13	7
Itzcuintli....	Quauhtli	Xochitl......	Coatl	2	9	3	10	4	11	5	12	6	13	7	1	8
Ozomatli.....	Coacaquauh-tli.	Cipactli......	Miquiztli....	3	10	4	11	5	12	6	13	7	1	8	2	9
Malinalli....	Ollin.......	Ehecatl	Mazatl......	4	11	5	12	6	13	7	1	8	2	9	3	10
Acatl	Tecpatl.....	Calli	Tochtli	5	12	6	13	7	1	8	2	9	3	10	4	11
Ocelotl......	Quiahuitl....	Cuetzpalin ..	Atl	6	13	7	1	8	2	9	3	10	4	11	5	12
Quauhtli.....	Xochitl	Coatl........	Itzcuintli....	7	1	8	2	9	3	10	4	11	5	12	6	13

This calendar begins the year Acatl with Cipactli to correspond with what I believe to have been the plan on which the Fejervary plate was made; this, as will be seen, does not agree with what is generally supposed to have been the usual method. The following table of days can be used for either year, but commences as the Acatl years in the preceding calendar.

TABLE XV.—A LIST OF MEXICAN DAYS FOR THIRTEEN MONTHS.

[The dark lines indicate the points where the months end.]

1. Dragon.	5. Flint.	9. Eagle.	13. Grass.
2. Wind.	6. Rain.	10. Vulture.	1. Cane.
3. House.	7. Flower.	11. Movement.	2. Tiger.
4. Lizard.	8. Dragon.	12. Flint.	3. Eagle.
5. Snake.	9. Wind.	13. Rain.	4. Vulture.
6. Death.	10. House.	1. Flower.	5. Movement.
7. Deer.	11. Lizard.	2. Dragon.	6. Flint.
8. Rabbit.	12. Snake.	3. Wind.	7. Rain.
9. Water.	13. Death.	4. House.	8. Flower.
10. Dog.	1. Deer.	5. Lizard.	9. Dragon.
11. Monkey.	2. Rabbit.	6. Snake.	10. Wind.
12. Grass.	3. Water.	7. Death.	11. House.
13. Cane.	4. Dog.	8. Deer.	12. Lizard.
1. Tiger.	5. Monkey.	9. Rabbit.	13. Snake.
2. Eagle.	6. Grass.	10. Water.	1. Death.
3. Vulture.	7. Cane.	11. Dog.	2. Deer.
4. Movement.	8. Tiger.	12. Monkey.	3. Rabbit.

4. Water.	10. Tiger.	3. Rain.	9. Lizard.
5. Dog.	11. Eagle.	4. Flower.	10. Snake.
6. Monkey.	12. Vulture.	5. Dragon.	11. Death.
7. Grass.	13. Movement.	6. Wind.	12. Deer.
8. Cane.	1. Flint.	7. House.	13. Rabbit.
9. Tiger.	2. Rain.	8. Lizard.	1. Water.
10. Eagle.	3. Flower.	9. Snake.	2. Dog.
11. Vulture.	4. Dragon.	10. Death.	3. Monkey.
12. Movement.	5. Wind.	11. Deer.	4. Grass.
13. Flint.	6. House.	12. Rabbit.	5. Cane.
1. Rain.	7. Lizard.	13. Water.	6. Tiger.
2. Flower.	8. Snake.	1. Dog.	7. Eagle.
3. Dragon.	9. Death.	2. Monkey.	8. Vulture.
4. Wind.	10. Deer.	3. Grass.	9. Movement.
5. House.	11. Rabbit.	4. Cane.	10. Flint.
6. Lizard.	12. Water.	5. Tiger.	11. Rain.
7. Snake.	13. Dog.	6. Eagle.	12. Flower.
8. Death.	1. Monkey.	7. Vulture.	13. Dragon.
9. Deer.	2. Grass.	8. Movement.	1. Wind.
10. Rabbit.	3. Cane.	9. Flint.	2. House.
11. Water.	4. Tiger.	10. Rain.	3. Lizard.
12. Dog.	5. Eagle.	11. Flower.	4. Snake.
13. Monkey.	6. Vulture.	12. Dragon.	5. Death.
1. Grass.	7. Movement.	13. Wind.	6. Deer.
2. Cane.	8. Flint.	1. House.	7. Rabbit.
3. Tiger.	9. Rain.	2. Lizard.	8. Water.
4. Eagle.	10. Flower.	3. Snake.	9. Dog.
5. Vulture.	11. Dragon.	4. Death.	10. Monkey.
6. Movement.	12. Wind.	5. Deer.	11. Grass.
7. Flint.	13. House.	6. Rabbit.	12. Cane.
8. Rain.	1. Lizard.	7. Water.	13. Tiger.
9. Flower.	2. Snake.	8. Dog.	1. Eagle.
10. Dragon.	3. Death.	9. Monkey.	2. Vulture.
11. Wind.	4. Deer.	10. Grass.	3. Movement.
12. House.	5. Rabbit.	11. Cane.	4. Flint.
13. Lizard.	6. Water.	12. Tiger.	5. Rain.
1. Snake.	7. Dog.	13. Eagle.	6. Flower.
2. Death.	8. Monkey.	1. Vulture.	7. Dragon.
3. Deer.	9. Grass.	2. Movement.	8. Wind.
4. Rabbit.	10. Cane.	3. Flint.	9. House.
5. Water.	11. Tiger.	4. Rain.	10. Lizard.
6. Dog.	12. Eagle.	5. Flower.	11. Snake.
7. Monkey.	13. Vulture.	6. Dragon.	12. Death.
8. Grass.	1. Movement.	7. Wind.	13. Deer.
9. Cane.	2. Flint.	8. House.	1. Rabbit.

2. Water.	5. Grass.	8. Eagle.	11. Flint.
3. Dog.	6. Cane.	9. Vulture.	12. Rain.
4. Monkey.	7. Tiger.	10. Movement.	13. Flower.

Although the Mexican equivalents of these names may be inferred from what has already been given, I will insert the Mexican and English names of the twenty days here, opposite each other.

TABLE XVI.

Mex.	Eng.	Mex.	Eng.
Cipactli (Dragon).		Ozomatli (Monkey).	
Ehecatl (Wind).		Malinalli (Grass).	
Calli (House).		Acatl (Cane).	
Cuetzpalin (Lizard).		Ocelotl (Tiger).	
Coatl (Snake).		Quauhtli (Eagle).	
Miquiztli (Death).		Cozcaquauhtli (Vulture).	
Mazatl (Deer).		Ollin (Movement).	
Tochtli (Rabbit).		Tecpatl (Flint).	
Atl (Water).		Quiahuitl (Rain).	
Itzcuintli (Dog).		Xochitl (Flower).	

Examining the looped line, Plate III, we notice at each of the outer and inner bends one of the day symbols. (In the plate of the Cortesian Codex there are two.) We therefore take for granted that this is the *first* day of the week, or indication of *thirteen days*, hence we should commence with Cipactli (or Dragon). This we find at the upper right hand corner of the inner square or right base of the large red loop. Judging from the direction of the birds' heads and other facts heretofore noted, we presume the direction in which we are to move is around toward the left. Counting the day symbol as one, and each of the twelve dots up the red line as one day, we come to the symbol in the upper right-hand corner of the loop as the first day of the next week. This we find is Ocelotl (Tiger), just as we find it to be in the calendar table and list of days. Moving along the upper red line to the corner at the left we find the next character is Mazatl (or Deer), agreeing exactly with the calendar and list. Moving down the left red line to the inner corner we come to the symbol for Xochitl (or Flower), also agreeing with the calendar and list. Proceeding from thence up the white line we reach next the symbol for the day Acatl (Cane) in the red circle surrounded by a yellow line. Here we see a marked distinction between this and the other day symbols we have named, a distinction which applies only to the four at the corners—the four year symbols—*Acatl, Tecpatl, Calli,* and *Tochtli.*

In order that the reader may compare the names in this looped line with the calendar, I present here a scheme of it similar to that given of

the plate from the Cortesian Codex.   The explanation given of the other
will enable him to make the comparison without further aid.

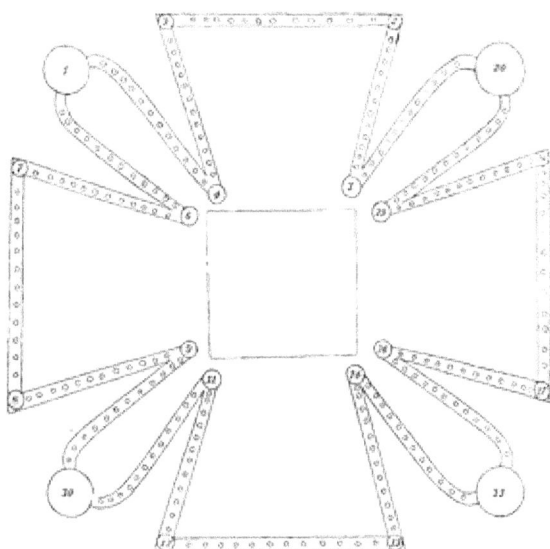

FIG. 6.—Scheme of Plate 44, Fejervary Codex.

The numbers in the little circles at the corners and loops replace the
days of the original as follows: 1, Cipactli; 2, Ocelotl; 3, Mazatl; 4,
Xochitl; 5, Acatl; 6, Miquiztli; 7, Quiahuitl; 8, Malinalli; 9, Coatl;
10, Tecpatl; 14, Ozomatli; 12, Cuetzpalin; 13, Ollin; 14, Itzcuintli; 15,
Calli; 16, Cozcaquauhtli; 17, Atl; 18, Ehecatl; 19, Quauhtli; 20, Tochtli.

As before stated, the four groups of five day symbols are found wedged
in between the loops at the corners.

In the upper left-hand corner we see the following: Cipactli, Acatl,
Coatl, Ollin, and Atl (or, to give the English equivalents in the same
order, Dragon, Cane, Snake, Movement, and Water), the same as those
of column 1 of Tables XI and XII.   In the lower left-hand corner,
Ehecatl, Itzcuintli, Tecpatl, Miquiztli, and Ocelotl (Wind, Dog. Flint,
Death, and Tiger), the same as column 2; in the lower right-hand
corner, Quauhtli, Calli, Ozomatli, Quiahuitl, and Mazatl (Eagle, House,
Monkey, Rain, and Deer), the same as column 3; and in the upper right-
hand corner, Tochtli, Cozcaquauhtli, Cuetzpalin, Malinalli, and Xochitl

(Rabbit, Vulture, Lizard, Grass, Flower), the same as column 4. But
the arrangement of the days in the respective columns, as in the "Table
of the Bacabs," varies from that obtained by placing the days of the
month in four groups, as heretofore explained.

Turning again to the plate of the Cortesian Codex, as shown in our
Plate 2, I call attention first to the heavy black L-shaped figures. I
presume from the number—eighteen—and the fact that they are found
in the line of weeks they are symbols of, or denote the months, but am
unable to suggest any explanation of their use in this connection. I
find nothing to correspond with them in either of the plates of the Mexican Codices referred to.

We are now prepared to enter upon the discussion of the symbols of the cardinal points, of which figures have already been given in connection with the quotations from Rosny's work (Fig. 1), but as I shall have occasion to refer to them very frequently I again present them in Fig. 7.

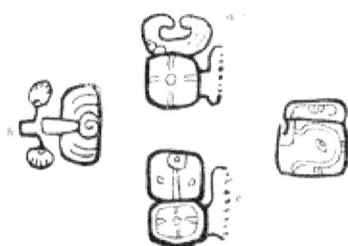

Fig. 7.—Symbols of the cardinal points.

As it is conceded by all who have discussed this subject, that *a* and *c* must be assigned to the east and west or equatorial points, the only dispute being as to which should be referred to the east and which to the west, it follows that the others must be referred to the polar points. As each one of the four areas or compartments contains one of these symbols—the top or upper compartment *a*, the left hand *b*, the bottom *c*, and the right-hand *d*—we naturally infer that the other figures in these compartments have some reference to the cardinal points with which they are respectively associated.

I think that Rosny is correct in assuming that this plate places these symbols in their proper positions, and hence that if we can determine one with satisfactory certainty this will determine the rest. If their correct positions are given anywhere it would seem that it would be here, in what is evidently a general calendar table or possibly a calendar wheel.

I have already discussed the question of the assignment of the cardinal symbols to some extent in my former work,[18] and will take for granted that the reader is familiar with what is there stated.

That one of the two characters *a* and *c* (Fig. 7), denotes the *east* or sunrise and the other *west* or sunset, may, I think, be safely assumed from what is given in the work mentioned, and from the evidence pre-

[18] Study Manuscript Troano, pp. 69-71.

sented by Rosuy,[15] and Schultz-Sellack.[16] But which east and which west is the rock on which the deductions have been, so far, split asunder; Rosuy and Schultz-Sellack maintaining that *a* is west and *c* east, and I that *a* is east and *c* west. If we admit that they are correctly placed on this plate it necessitates the admission on my part that I have been incorrect in my reference of two of them. If *a* is east then I have reversed those denoting north and south; if it is west, then I was correct as to those denoting north and south, but have reversed those indicating east and west.

Without at present stating the result of my re-examination of this subject I shall enter at once upon the discussion, leaving this to appear as we proceed.

It is well known that each of the dominical days or year-bearers (*Cuch-haab*, as they were termed by the Mayas), Kan, Muluc, Ix, and Cauac, was referred to one of the four cardinal points. Our first step, therefore, is to determine the points to which these days were respectively assigned.

I have given in my former paper[17] my reasons for believing that Cauac was referred to the south, Kan to the east, Muluc to the north, and Ix to the west, from which I quote the following as a basis for further argument:

"Landa, Cogulludo, and Perez tell us that each of the four dominical days was referred by the Indians to one of the four cardinal points. As the statements of these three authorities appear at first sight to conflict with each other, let us see if we can bring them into harmony without resorting to a violent construction of the language used. Perez' statement is clear and distinct, and as it was made by one thoroughly conversant with the manners and customs of the natives, and also with all the older authorities, it is doubtless correct.

"He says, 'The Indians made a little wheel in which they placed the initial days of the year. *Kan* at the *east*, *Muluc* at the *north*, *Gix* or *Hix* at the *west*, and *Cauac* at the *south*, to be counted in the same order.'

"The statement of Cogulludo, which agrees substantially with this, is as follows : 'They fixed the first year at the east, to which they gave the name *Cuch-haab* ; the second at the west, and called it *Hiix* ; the the third at the south, named *Cauac*, and the fourth, *Muluc*, at the north.'

"Turning now to Landa's work (*Relac. de las Cosas*, §§ XXXIV), we are somewhat surprised to find the following language: 'The first of these dominical letters is *Kan*. * * * They placed this on the south side. * * * The second letter is *Muluc*, which is placed on the eastern side. * * * The third of these letters is *Yx*, * * * and it signi-

[15] Les. Doc. Ecrit. l'Antiq. Ameriq.
[16] Zeits. für Etho., 1879.
[17] Study Manuscript Troano, pp. 66-70.

ned the northern side. The fourth letter is *Cauac*, which is assigned to the western side.'

"This, as we see, places Kan at the south, Muluc at the east, Ix at the north, and Cauac at the west, conflicting directly with the statements made by Cogulludo and Perez. If we turn now to the description of the four feasts as given by Landa, and heretofore quoted, I think we shall find an explanation of this difference. From his account of the feast at the commencement of the Kan year (the intercalated days of the Cauac year) we learn that first they made an idol called *Kan-u-uayeyab*, which they bore to the heap of stones on the south side of the village; next they made a statue of the god *Bolon-Zacab*, which they placed in the house of the elected chief, or chief chosen for the occasion. This done they returned to the idol on the southern stone heap, where certain religious ceremonies were performed, after which they returned with the idol to the house, where they placed it *vis-a-vis* with the other, just as we see in the lower division of Plates XX–XXIII of the Manuscript Troano. Here they kept constant vigil until the unlucky days (*Uayeyab-haab*) had expired and the new Kan year appeared; then they took the statue of *Bolon-Zacab* to the temple and the other idol to the heap of stones at the *east* side of the village, where it was to remain during the year, doubtless intended as a constant reminder to the common people of what year was passing.

"Similar transfers were made at the commencement of the other years; at that of Muluc, first to the east, then to the house, and then to its final resting place on the *north* side; of Ix, first to the north, then to the *west ;* of Cauac, first to the west, then to the *south*.

"This movement agrees precisely with the order given by Perez; the final resting places of their idols for the year being the cardinal points of the dominical days where he fixes them; that is, Kan at the *east*, Muluc at the *north*, Ix at the *west*, and Cauac at the *south*. There is, therefore, no real disagreement between these authorities on this point."

Most of the modern authors who have touched upon this topic, although in some cases apparently at sea, without any fixed opinion on the subject, are disposed to follow Landa's statement, without comparing it with his account of the supplemental days, and appear to rely upon it rather than upon the statements of Cogulludo and Perez; and hence they refer Kan to the south, Muluc to the east, Ix to the north, and Cauac to the west.

Brasseur, in his *Histoire des Nations civilisées du Mexique et de l'Amérique Centrale*,[18] assigns Kan to the east, Muluc to the north, Hix to the west, and Cauac to the south. But in his supplement to *Études sur le Manuscrit Troano*,[19] and in his note to Landa's *Relacion*,[20] refers Kan to the south, Muluc to the east, Ix to the north, and Cauac to the west,

---

[18] Vol. III, p. 474.   [19] P. 234.   [20] P. 209.

although afterwards, in the same work, in a note to Perez' *Cronologia*, he quotes Cogulludo's statement without explanation or objection.

Dr. Brinton, in his *Myths of the New World*,[21] places these dominical days at the same points to which I have assigned them—Kan at the east, &c.—although referring in a note at the same place to the very page of Landa's *Relacion*, where they are assigned as given by Rosny. In a subsequent work, *Hero Myths*, referring to the same passage in Landa, and with Cogulludo's work before him, he assigns them to the same points as Rosny—Kan to the south, &c.—yet without any reference whatever to his former expressed opinion.

Schultz-Sellack, in an article entitled *Die Amerikanischen Gotter der vier Weltrichtungen und ihre Tempel in Palenque*, in the *Zeitschrift für Ethnologie* for 1879,[22] comes to the same conclusion as Rosny.

Rosny's opinion on this subject has already been quoted.[23]

From these facts it is evident that the assignment of the dominical days to their respective cardinal points has not as yet been satisfactorily determined, but that the tendency at the present day is to follow Landa's simple statement rather than Cogulludo and Perez. This is caused, I presume, in part, by the fact that certain colors—yellow, red, white, and black—were also referred to the cardinal points, and because it is supposed that among the Maya nations yellow was appropriated to Kan, red to Muluc, white to Ix, and black to Cauac; and as the first appears to be more appropriate to the south, red to the east or sunrise, white to the north or region of snow, and black to the west or sunset, therefore this is the correct assignment.

But there is nothing given to show that this was the reason for the selection or reference of these colors by the inhabitants of Central America.

This brings another factor into the discussion and widens the field of our investigation; and as but little, save the terms applied to or connected with the dominical days, is to be found in regard to the Maya custom in this respect, we are forced to refer to the Mexican custom as the next best evidence. But it is proper to state first that the chief, and, so far as I am aware, the only, authority for the reference of the colors named to the four Maya days, is found in the names applied to them by Landa.[24]

According to this writer, the other names applied to the *Bacab* of Kan, were *Hobnil*, *Kanil-Bacab*, *Kan-Pauahtun*, and *Kan-Xib-Chac*; to that of Muluc, *Canzienal*, *Chacal-Bacab*, *Chac-Pauahtun*, and *Chac-Xib-Chac*; to that of Ix, *Zac-Ziui*, *Zacal-Bacab*, *Zac-Pauahtun*, and *Zac-Xib-Chac*; and to that of Cauac, *Hozen-Ek*, *Ekel-Bacab*, *Ek-Pauahtun*, and *Ek-Xib-Chac.* As Kan or Kanil of the first signifies *yellow*, Chac or Chacal of the second signifies *red*, Zac or Zacal, of the third *white*, and Ek or Ekel,

---

[21] P. 82.   [23] See also hisDeehiff. Ecrit. Hierat., p. 42.

[22] P. 209.   [24] Relacion, p.208.

of the fourth *black*, it has been assumed, and, I think, correctly, that these colors were usually referred to these days, or rather to the cardinal points indicated, respectively, by these day symbols. If there is any other authority for this conclusion in the works of the earlier writers, I have so far been unable to find it.

If the figures in our plate are properly and distinctly colored in the original Codex Cortesianus, this might form one aid in settling this point, but, as we shall hereafter see, the colors really afford very little assistance, as they are varied for different purposes.

Rosny gives us no information on this point, hence our discussion must proceed without this knowledge, as we have no opportunity of referring to the original. I may remark that it is the opinion of the artist, Mr. Holmes, from an inspection of the photograph, that the plate was at least partially colored.

M. de Charencey, who has studied with much care the custom of identifying colors with the cardinal points in both the New and Old World, believes that in Mexico and Central America the original system was to refer yellow to the east, black to the north, white to the west, and red to the south.[25]

When we turn to the Mexican system we find the data greatly increased, but, unfortunately, the difficulties and confusion are increased in like proportion. Here we have not only the four dominical days and the four colors, but also the four ages, four elements, and four seasons, all bearing some relation in this system to the four cardinal points. It will be necessary, therefore, for us to carry along with us these several ideas in our attempt to arrive at a satisfactory conclusion on this complicated and mystified subject.

Before referring to the codices I will present the conclusions of the principal authorities who have devoted any attention to this question. Sahagun says, "The names that they gave to the four parts of the earth are these: Vitzlampa, the south; Tlapcopcopa, the east; Mictlampa, the north; Coatlampa, the west. The names of the figures dedicated to these parts are these: Tochtli, the rabbit, was dedicated to Vitzlampa, the south; Acatl, the cane, to the east; Tecpatl, the flint, to the north; Calli, the house, to the west; * * * * and at the end of fifty-two years the count came back to *Cetochtlincatl*, which is the figure of the reed, dedicated to the east, which they called *Tlapcopcopa* and *Tlavilcopa*, nearly towards the fire or the sun. Tecpatl, which is the figure of a flint, was dedicated to Mictlampa, nearly towards hell, because

---

[25] *Des couleurs considérées comme Symboles des Points de l'Horizon chez des Peuples du Noveau Monde*, in *Actes de la Societe Philologique*, tome VI. See also his *Recherches sur les Noms des Points de l'Espace*, in *Mem. Acad. Nat. Sci. et Arts et Belles Lettres de Caen*, 1882.

Since the above was written I have received a copy of his *Ages ou Soleils*, in which he gives the Mexican custom of assigning the colors as follows: blue to the south, red to the east, yellow to the north, and green to the west.—P. 40.

they believed that the dead went towards the north. For which reason, in the superstition which represented the dead as covered with
mantas (cloths) and their bodies bound, they made them sit with their
faces turned toward the north, or Mictlampa. The fourth figure was
the house, and was dedicated to the west, which they called Cioatlampa,
which is nearly toward the house of the women, for they held the opinion that the dead women, who are goddesses, live in the west, and that
the dead men, who are in the house of the sun, guide him from the east
with rejoicings every day, until they arrive at midday, and that the defunct women, whom they regard as goddesses, and call Cioapipiltin,
come out from the west to receive him at midday and carry him with
rejoicing to the west."[35]

Veytia's statement in regard to the same subject is as follows:

"The symbols, then, which were used in the aforesaid monarchies for
the numeration of their years were these four: Tecpatl, that signifies
flint; Calli, the house; Tochtli, the rabbit; and Acatl, the reed.
* * * The material signification of the names are those just
given, but the allegories that they wished to set forth by them are the
four elements, which they understood to be the origin of all composite
matter, and into which all things could be resolved.

"They gave to fire the first place, as the most noble of all, and symbolized it by the flint. * * * By the hieroglyphic of 'the house'
they represent the element earth, and gave it the second place in their
initial characters.

"By the rabbit they symbolized the air, * * * and represented
it in various ways, among which was the sign of the holy cross. * * *

"Finally the fourth initial character, which is the reed, which is the
proper meaning of the word Acatl, is the hieroglyphic of the element
water.'[36]

At page 48: "It is to be noted that most of the old calendars—those
of the cycles as well as those of years and months, which they used to
form in circles and squares, ran from the right to the left, in the way
the orientals write and not as we are accustomed to form such figures.
* * * But they did not maintain this order in the figures that they
painted and used as hieroglyphics in them, but placed them some looking
to one side and some to the other."

Gemelli Carreri[38] writes as follows in regard to the Mexican calendar
system:

"A snake turned itself round into a circle and in the body of the
serpent there were four divisions. The first denoted the south, in that
language call'd Uatzlampa, whose hieroglyphick was a rabbit in a blew
field, which they called Tochtli. Lower was the part that signify'd the
east, called Tlacopa or Tlahuilcopa, denoted by a cane in a red field,

[35] Hist. Gen. de las Cosas de Nueva Espana, tome 2, p. 256.
[37] Hist. Ant. Mex., vol. 1, p. 42.
[38] Churchill's Voyages, vol. IV, pp. 491, 492.

call'd *Acatl*. The hieroglyphick of the north, or *Micolampa*, was a sword pointed with flint, call'd *Tecpatl*, in a yellow field. That of the west or *Sihuatlampa*, was a house in a green field, and called *Cagli.* * * *

"These four divisions were the beginning of the four terms that made up the age. Between every two on the inside of the snake were twelve small divisions, among which the four first names or figures were successively distributed, giving every one its number to thirteen, which was the number of years that composed an indication; the like was done in the second indication with the same names from one to thirteen, and so in the third and fourth, till they finished the circle of fifty-two years. * * * From what has been said above, there arise several doubts; the first is, why they begin to reckon their years from the south; the second, why they made use of the four figures, of a rabbit, a cane, a flint, and a house."

He then goes on to state that the Mexicans believed the sun or light first appeared in the south, and that hell or inferno was in the north; then adds the following:

"Having found this analogy between the age and the year, they would carry the similitude or proportions on further, and, as in the year there are four seasons, so they would adapt the like to the age, and accordingly they appointed *Tochtli* for its beginning in the south, as it were, the spring and youth of the sun's age; *Acatl* for the summer, *Tecpatl* for the autumn, and *Cagli* for his old age or winter.

"These figures so disposed were also the hieroglyphicks of the elements, which is the second doubt; for *Tochtli* was dedicated to *Teacayohua*, god of earth; *Acatl* to *Tlalocatetuhtli*, god of water; *Tecpatl* to *Chetzalcoatl*, god of air; and *Cagli* to *Xiuhtecuhil*, god of fire. * * *

"The days *Cipactli*, *Michitzli*, *Ozomatli*, and *Cozcaquauhtli* are companions to—that is, in all respects follow—the order of the four figures that denote the years of an age, viz, *Tochtli*, *Acatl*, *Tecpatl*, and *Cagli*, to signify that every year whose symbol is *Tochtli* will have *Cipactli* for the first day of the month; that whose symbol or distinctive mark is *Acatl* will have *Michitzli* for the first of the month; *Tecpatl* will have *Ozomatli*, and *Cagli* will have *Cozcaquauhtli*."

Clavigero[20] agrees with Gemelli in reference to the correspondence of the year symbols with the first days of the years, and inserts the following remark in a note:

"Cav. Boturini says that the year of the rabbet began uniformly with the day of the rabbet, the year of the cane with the day of the cane, &c., and never with the days which we have mentioned; but we ought to give more faith to Siguenza, who was certainly better informed in Mexican antiquity. The system of this gentleman is fantastical and full of contradictions."

From this statement we infer that Siguenza held the same opinion on this point as Clavigero and Gemelli.

---

[20] Hist. Mex. Cullen's Transl., I, 292.

Boturini[30] gives the following arrangement of the "symbols of the four parts or angles of the world," comparing it with that of Gemelli.

"Gemelli.	"Boturini.
1. Tochtli = South.	1. Tecpatl = South.
2. Acatl = East.	2. Calli = East.
3. Tecpatl = North.	3. Tochtli = North.
4. Calli = West."	4. Acatl = West."

SYMBOLS OF THE FOUR ELEMENTS.

"Gemelli.	"Boturini.
1. Tochtli = Earth.	1. Tecpatl = Fire.
2. Acatl = Water.	2. Calli = Earth.
3. Tecpatl = Air.	3. Tochtli = Air.
4. Calli = Fire."	4. Acatl = Water."

Herrera speaks only of the year symbols and colors, and, although he does not directly connect them, indicates his understanding in regard thereto by the order in which he mentions them :[31]

"They divided the year into four signs, being four figures, the one of a house, another of a rabbit, the third of a cane, the fourth of a flint, and by them they reckoned the year as it passed on, saying, such a thing happened at so many houses or at so many flints of such a wheel or rotation, because their life being as it were an age, contained four weeks of years consisting of thirteen, so that the whole made up fifty-two years. They painted a sun in the middle from which issued four lines or branches in a cross to the circumference of the wheel, and they turned so that they divided it into four parts, and the circumference and each of them moved with its branch of the same color, which were four, *Green*, *Blue*, *Red*, and *Yellow*; and each of those parts had thirteen subdivisions with the sign of a house, a rabbit, a cane, or a flint."

From this statement I presume his arrangement would be as follows:

Calli — Green.
Tochtli — Blue.
Acatl — Red.
Tecpatl — Yellow.

Still, this is at best but a supposition. It is evident that he had before him or referred to a wheel similar to that figured by Duran in his *Historia de las Indias*, as his description agrees with it in every respect, except as to the arrangement of the colors.

According to Duran[32] "The circle was divided into four parts, each part containing thirteen years, the first part pertaining to the east, the second to the north, the third to the west, and the fourth to the south.

[30] *Idea de Una Nueva Historia General de la America Septentrional*, pp. 54-56.
[31] Hist. Amer. Dec. II, B. 10, Chap. 4. Transl. vol. 3, pp. 221-222.
[32] *Historia de las Indias de Nueva Espana, Mexico*, 1880. Tom. II., pp 252-253.

The first part, which pertained to the east, was called the thirteen years of the *Cane*, and in each house of the thirteen was painted a cane, and the number of the corresponding year. * * * The second part applied to the north, in which were other thirteen houses (divisions), called the thirteen houses of the *Flint*, and there were also painted in each one a flint and the number of the year. * * * The third part, that which appertained to the west, was called the thirteen *Houses*; there were also painted in this thirteen little houses, and joined to each the number of the year. * * * In the fourth and last part were other thirteen years called the thirteen houses of the *Rabbit*, and in each of these houses were also likewise painted the head of a rabbit, and joined to it a number."

The plate or figure accompanying this statement" is a wheel in the form shown in Fig. 8, the quadrant *a* green, with thirteen figures of the

Fɪɢ. 8—Calendar wheel from Duran.

cane in it; *b* red, with thirteen figures of the flint in it; *c* yellow with thirteen figures of the house in it, and *d* blue, with thirteen figures of the rabbit's head in it, each figure with its appropriate numeral. At the top is the word "Oriente," at the left "Norte," at the bottom "Occidente," and at the right "Sur."

Although this figure was evidently made by this author or for him, it expresses his understanding of the assignment of the years and arrangement of the colors as ascertained from the data accessible to him.

His arrangement will therefore be as follows:

Acatl — East — Green.
Tecpatl— North — Red.
Calli — West — Yellow.
Tochtli — South — Blue.

We find the same idea frequently expressed in the codices now accessible, as, for example, the Borgian and the Vatican B, though the colors do not often correspond with Duran's arrangement.

Shultz-Sellack,[24] in his article heretofore quoted, arranges the colors in connection with the dominical days in the Maya system as follows:

Kan   — South — Yellow.
Muluc — East — Red.
Ix   — North — White.
Canac — West — Black.

He does not appear to be so clear in reference to the Mexican system, in fact he seems to avoid the question of the assignment of the year symbols. His arrangement, as far as I can understand it, is as follows:

— ? Quetzalcoatl — South — Wind — Yellow.
— ? Huitzilopuchtli — East — Fire — Red.
— ? Tezcatlipoca   — North — Water — White.
— ? Tlaloc   — West — Earth — Black.

Orozco y Berra[25] gives his preference to the opinion of Sahagun, which has already been quoted, and which is the same as that held by Torquemada.[26]

The most thorough and extensive discussion of this subject which has so far been made, is by Dr. D. Alfredo Chavero, in the *Anales del Musco Nacional de Mexico*.[27]

According to this author, who had access not only to the older as well as more recent authorities usually referred to, but also to the manuscript of Fabrigat and the Codex Chimalpopoca or Quauhtitlan, the order of the year symbols or year bearers—Tecpatl, Calli, Acatl, and Tochtli—varied "*segun les pueblos*," the Toltecs commencing the cycle with *Tecpatl*, those of Teotihuacan with *Calli*, those of Tezcuco with

---

[24] Zeit. für Ethnologie, 1879.
[25] Anales Mus. Mex., I, Entrag. 7, p. 299.
[26] Monarq. Indiana, lib. X, cap. 36.
[27] Tom. 1, Entrag. 7, tom. II, and continued in tom. III.

Acatl, and the Mexicans with *Tochtli*.[26] He also shows that the relation and order of the four ages or creations and elements in regard to the cardinal points, are by no means uniform, not only in the Spanish and early authorities, but in the codices and monuments (supposing his interpretation to be correct).

His arrangement, as derived from the leading codices, is as follows:

```
          Tochtli — South — Earth.
          Acatl  — East  — Water.
          Tecpatl — North — Fire.
          Calli  — West  — Air.
```

In order that the various views may be seen at a glance, I give here a tabulated *résumé*:

MEXICAN SYMBOLS OF THE CARDINAL POINTS.

Veytia.

```
          1. Tecpatl — Flint   — Fire.
          2. Calli   — House  — Earth.
          3. Tochtli — Rabbit — Air.
          4. Acatl   — Cane   — Water.
```

Sahagun.

```
     1. Tochtli — Rabbit — South.
     2. Acatl   — Cane   — East.  "Toward the fire or sun."
     3. Tecpatl — Flint  — North. "Nearly towards hell."
     4. Calli   — House  — West.  "Towards the house of women."
```

Gemelli.

```
1. Tochtli — Rabbit — South — Blue   — Earth — Cipactli.
2. Acatl   — Cane   — East  — Red    — Water — Michiztli.
3. Tecpatl — Flint  — North — Yellow — Air   — Ozomatli.
4. Calli   — House  — West  — Green  — Fire  — Cozcaqnauhtli.
```

Boturini.

```
          1. Tecpatl — Flint  — South — Fire.
          2. Calli   — House  — East  — Earth.
          3. Tochtli — Rabbit — North — Air.
          4. Acatl   — Cane   — West  — Water.
```

Herrera.

```
          Calli   — House  — Green.
          Tochtli — Rabbit — Blue.
          Acatl   — Cane   — Red.
          Tecpatl — Flint  — Yellow.
```

---

[26] A fact mentioned by Leon y Gama (Dos Piedras, pt. I, p. 16), and Veytia (Hist. Antiq. Mej., tom. I, p. 58). See, also, Müller, *Reisen*, tom. III, p. 65, and Boturini, Idea, p. 127.

Duran.

1. Acatl   — Cane   — East   — Green.
2. Tecpatl — Flint — North — Red.
3. Calli   — House — West   — Yellow.
4. Tochtli — Rabbit— South — Blue.

Schultz-Sellack.

1.— ? — Quetzalcoatl — South — Wind — Yellow.
2.— ? — Huitzilopuchtli — East   — Fire — Red.
3.— ? — Tezcatlipoca   — North — Water — White.
4.— ? — Tlaloc   — West   — Earth — Black.

Charencey.

1.— ? — East   — Yellow.
2.— ? — North — Black.
3.— ? — West — White.
4.— ? — South — Red.[29]

Orozco y Berra.

1. Tochtli — Rabbit — South — Air.
2. Acatl   — Cane   — East   — Water.
3. Tecpatl — Flint   — North — Fire.
4. Calli   — House   — West   — Earth.

Charero.

1. Tochtli — Rabbit — South — Earth.
2. Acatl   — Cane   — East   — Water.
3. Tecpatl — Flint   — North — Fire.
4. Calli   — House — West   — Air.

Judging from the differences shown in these lists, we are forced to the conclusion that no entirely satisfactory result has been reached in reference to the assignment of the different symbols to the cardinal points; still a careful analysis will bring out the fact that there is a strong prevalency of opinion on one or two points among the earlier authorities. In order that this may be seen I present here a list in a different form from the preceding.

---

[29] I see from Charencey's *"Ages ou Soleils,"* just received, that he concludes the arrangement by the Mexicans was as follows:

1. Tochtli — Rabbit — Blue   — Earth — South.
2. Acatl   — Cane   — Red   — Water — East.
3. Tecpatl — Flint   — Yellow — Air   — North.
4. Calli   — House — Green — Fire   — West.

REFERENCE OF THE YEARS TO THE CARDINAL POINTS.

	Tochtli —	Acatl —	Tecpatl —	Calli
Sahagun	— South	— East	— North	— West.
Gemelli	— South	— East	— North	— West.
Duran	— South	— East	— North	— West.
Orozco y Berra	— South	— East	— North	— West.
Chavero	— South	— East	— North	— West.
Torquemada	— South	— East	— North	— West.
Boturini	— North	— West	— South	— East.

REFERENCE OF COLORS TO THE CARDINAL POINTS.

	South	— East	— North	— West.
Gemelli	— Blue	— Red	— Yellow	— Green.
Duran	— Blue	— Green	— Red	— Yellow.
Charencey[30]	— Red	— Yellow	— Black	— White.
Schultz Sellack	— Yellow	— Red	— White	— Black.

REFERENCE OF ELEMENTS TO THE CARDINAL POINTS.

	South	— East	— North	— West.
Gemelli	— Earth	— Water	— Air[31]	— Fire.
Boturini	— Fire	— Earth	— Air	— Water.
Schultz Sellack	— Air	— Fire	— Water	— Earth.
Chavero	— Earth	— Water	— Fire	— Air.

REFERENCE OF THE ELEMENTS TO THE YEARS.

	Tochtli —	Acatl	— Tecpatl —	Calli
Veytia	— Air	— Water	— Fire	— Earth.
Gemelli	— Earth	— Water	— Air	— Fire.
Boturini	— Air	— Water	— Fire	— Earth.
Chavero	— Earth	— Water	— Fire	— Air.
Orozco y Berra	— Air	— Water	— Fire	— Earth.

As will be seen from this list, there is entire uniformity in the assignment of the years or year symbols to the cardinal points, with the single exception of Boturini. As this author's views in regard to the calendar are so radically different from all other authorities as to induce the belief that it applies to some other than the Aztec or true Mexican calendar we will probably be justified in eliminating his opinion from the discussion.

Omitting this author, we have entire uniformity among the authorities named in regard to the reference of the years to the cardinal points, as follows:

Tochtli to the *south*; *Acatl* to the *east*; *Tecpatl* to the *north*, and *Calli* to the *west*.

---

[30] See note 29 on page 47.

[31] By "air" in this connection "wind" is really intended.

The reference of the colors and the elements to the cardinal points is too varied to afford us any assistance in arriving at a conclusion in this respect. In the assignment of the elements to the years we find that water is referred by all the authorities named to *Acatl*, and fire by all but one (Gemelli), to *Tecpatl*.

One thing more must be mentioned before we appeal directly to the codices. As the groups of five days, so often heretofore referred to, were assigned to the cardinal points, it is proper to notice here what is said on this point. So far, I have found it referred to only in the Exposition of the Vatican Codex and by Schultz-Sellack in the article before cited.

As the latter refers to them by numbers only, I give here a list of the Mexican days, with numbers corresponding with the positions they severally hold in their regular order.

First column.	Second column.	Third column.	Fourth column.
1. Cipactli.	2. Ehecatl.	3. Calli.	4. Cuetzpalin.
5. Coatl.	6. Miquitzli.	7. Mazatl.	8. Tochtli.
9. Atl.	10. Itzquintli.	11. Ozomatli.	12. Malinalli.
13. Acatl.	14. Oceloti.	15. Quauhtli.	16. Cozcaquauhtli.
17. Ollin.	18. Tecpatl.	19. Quiahuitl.	20. Xochitl.

Using the numbers only, 1, 5, 9, 13, and 17 will denote the first column; 2, 6, 10, 14, and 18 the second, &c.

Schultz-Sellack states that:

4, 8, 12, 16, 20 were assigned to the south.

1, 5, 9, 13, 17, to the east.

2, 6, 10, 14, 18, to the north.

3, 7, 11, 15, 19, to the west.

But, as he only quotes from the explanation of the Vatican Codex as given by Kingsborough,[42] I will present here the statement of this authority:

"Thus they commenced reckoning from the sign of One Cane. For example: One Cane, two, three, &c., proceeding to thirteen; for, in the same way, as we have calculations in our repertories by which to find what sign rules over each of the seven days of the week, so the natives of that country had thirteen signs for the thirteen days of their week; and this will be better understood by an example. To signify the first day of the world, they painted a figure like the moon, surrounded with splendor, which is emblematical of the deliberation which they say their god held respecting the creation, because the first day after the commencement of time began with the second figure, which was One Cane. Accordingly, completing their reckoning of a cycle at the sign of Two Canes, they counted an Age, which is a period of fifty-two years, because,

---

[42] Kingsborough, vol. VI, pp. 196, 197.

on account of the bissextile years which necessarily fell in this sign of
the Cane, it occurred at the expiration of every period of fifty-two years.
Their third sign was a certain figure which we shall presently see, re-
sembling a serpent or viper, by which they intended to signify the pov-
erty and labors which men suffer in this life. Their fourth sign represented an earthquake, which they called Nahuolin, because they say
that in that sign the sun was created. Their fifth sign was Water, for,
according to their account, abundance was given to them in that
sign. [The five days Cipactli, Acatl, Coatl, Ollin, Atl.] These five
signs they placed in the upper part, which they called Tlacpac,
that is to say, the east. They placed five other signs at the south,
which they named Uitzlan, which means a place of thorns—the first of
which was a flower, emblematical of the shortness of life, which passes
away quickly, like a blossom or flower. The second was a certain very
green herb, in like manner denoting the shortness of life, which is as
grass. The third sign was a lizard, to show that the life of man, besides being brief, is destitute, and replete with the ills of nakedness and
cold, and with other miseries. The fourth was a certain very cruel spe-
cies of bird which inhabits that country. The fifth sign was a rabbit,
because they say that in this sign their food was created, and accordingly
they believed that it presided over drunken revels [Xochitl, Malinalli,
Cuetzpalin, Cozcaquauhtli, Tochtli.] They placed five other signs
at the west, which region they called Tetziuatlan. The first was a
deer, by which they indicated the diligence of mankind in seeking
the necessaries of life for their sustenance. The second sign was a
shower of rain falling from the skies, by which they signified pleasure
and worldly content. The third sign was an ape, denoting leisure
time. The fourth was a house, meaning repose and tranquillity. The
fifth was an eagle, the symbol of freedom and dexterity. [Mazatl,
Quiahuitl, Ozomatli, Calli, Quauhtli.] At the north, which they
call Teutletlapan, which signifies the place of the gods, they placed
the other five signs which were wanting to complete the twenty.
The first was a tiger, which is a very ferocious animal, and accordingly
they considered the echo of the voice as a bad omen and the most unlucky of any, because they say that it has reference to that sign. The
second was a skull or death, by which they signified that death commenced with the first existence of mankind. The third sign was a razor
or stone knife, by which are meant the wars and dissensions of the
world; they call it Tecpatl. The fourth sign is the head of a cane,
which signifies the devil, who takes souls to hell. The fifth and last of
all the twenty signs was a winged head, by which they represented the
wind, indicative of the variety of worldly affairs." [Ocelotl, Miquiztli,
Tecpatl, Itzquintli, Ehecatl.]

According, therefore, to this author the first column was assigned to
the East, the second to the North, the third to the West, and the fourth

to the South.   He also says that the counting of the years began with
1 Cane.[41]

Turning now to Plate 44 of the Fejervary Codex (our Plate III), we
notice that the symbols of the days of the first column are wedged in
between the loops of the upper left-hand corner, and that here we also
find the symbol of the year-bearer, *Acatl*, in the red circle at the outer
extremity of the loop. Here, then, according to the expounder of the
Vatican Codex, is the east, and this agrees also with all the other authorities except Boturini. As these day symbols are between the red
and yellow loops, the next point to be determined is to which of the
two they belong.

This is a very important point, the determination of which must have
a strong bearing on our decision as to the cardinal points. As it is here
that the apparently strongest evidence against my conclusion is to be
found, it is necessary that I explain somewhat fully my reasons for de-
ciding against this apparent evidence.

If we take for granted that the day columns relate to the large angular loops, then the column in the upper right-hand corner would seem
to belong to the top or red loop and not to the one on the right; and
the column in the upper left-hand corner to the left or yellow loop and
not to that at the top, and so on. This I concede is a natural inference
which it is necessary to outweigh by stronger evidence.

In the first place it is necessary to bear in mind that although the
sides of the plate, that is to say the large loops, are spoken of as facing
the cardinal points, yet it is possible the artist intended that the corner
or round loops should indicate the cardinal points, as here are found the
days assigned to these quarters.

Even admitting that the large angular loops indicate the cardinal
points, we must suppose the figures of one corner, either those at the
right or left, belong respectively to them. As the symbols of the year-
bearers Acatl, Tecpatl, Calli, and Tochtli have peculiar marks of distinction, we are justified in believing that this distinction is for the
purpose of signifying the quarter to which they belong. Examining
carefully the bird on the symbol for Acatl in the upper left-hand corner
loop, we find that it can be identified only with that on the tree in the
top or red angular loop. It is true the identification in the other cases
is not so certain, but in this case there can be very little doubt, as the
green top-knot, the peculiar beak, and green feathers are sufficient of
themselves to connect the upper left-hand white loop and figures of
this corner with the top red loop and figures embraced in it.

Studying the plate carefully and also our scheme of it—Fig. 6—we
observe that Cipactli is found at the right base of the red loop, Miquiztli
at the right base of the yellow loop (the center of the plate being considered the point of observation), Ozomatli at the right base of the blue

---

loop, and Cozcaquauhtli at the right base of the green loop (but in this case it can be determined only by the order, not by the figure). These are the four days, as is well known, on which the Mexican years begin.

I take for granted, therefore, that the year *Acatl* or Cane applies to the top or red loop. This, I am aware, necessitates commencing the year with 1 Cipactli, thus apparently contradicting the statement of Gemelli that the Tochtli year began with Cipactli. But it must be borne in mind that this author expressly proceeds upon the theory that the counting of the years began in the south with Tochtli. If the count began with 1 Cane, as both the expounder of the Vatican Codex and Duran affirm, Cipactli would be the first day of this year, as it appears evident from the day lists in the Codices that the first year of all the systems commenced with this day. That Acatl was assigned to the east is affirmed by all authorities save Boturini, and this agrees very well with the plate now under consideration. There is one statement made by the expounder of the Vatican Codex which not only enables us to understand his confused explanation, but indicates clearly the kind of painting he had in view, and tends to confirm the opinion here advanced.

He says that "to signify the first day of the world they painted a figure like the moon," &c. Let us guess this to be Cipactli, as nothing of the kind named is to be found. The next figure was a cane; their third figure was a serpent ; their fourth, earthquake (Ollin) ; their fifth, water. "These five signs they placed in the *upper part*, which they called *Tlacpac*, that is to say, the *east*." That he does not mean that these days followed each other consecutively in counting time must be admitted. That he saw them placed in this order in some painting may be inferred with positive certainty. It is also apparent that they are the five days of the first column in the arrangement of the Mexican days shown in Table No. XI, though not in the order there given, which is as follows:

Dragon, Snake, Water, Cane, Movement.

The order in which they are placed by this author is this :

Dragon? Cane, Serpent, Movement, Water.

Which, by referring to page 35, we find to be precisely the same as that of the five days wedged in between the loops in the *upper left*-hand corner of Plate 44 of the Fejervary Codex ; thus agreeing in order and position with this author's statement. Duran, as we have seen, also places the east at the top. The same thing is true in regard to the calendar wheel from the book of Chilan Balam hereafter shown.

Accordingly, I conclude that the top of this plate—the red loop—will be east ; the left-hand or yellow loop, north; the bottom or blue loop, west, and the right-hand or green loop, south. This also brings the year Acatl to the east, Tecpatl to the north, Calli to the west, and Tochtli to the south. As the commencement was afterwards changed to Tochtli, as we are informed by Chavero (and as appears to be the case in the Borgian Codex), it would begin at the south, just as stated by Gemelli and other early writers, who probably refer to the system in vogue at the time of the conquest.

Shultz-Sellack alludes to this plate in his article heretofore quoted, but considers the red loop the south, notwithstanding his assignment of red among the Aztecs to the east. He was led to this conclusion, I presume, by two facts: First, the close proximity of the fourth column of days to this red loop, and second, the figure of the sun at the foot of the tree or cross, the sun of the first creation having made its appearance, according to Mexican mythology, in the south. But it is far more likely that the artist intended here to be true to known phenomena rather than to a tradition which was in contradiction to them. The presence of this figure *above* the horizon is, I think, one of the strongest possible proofs that this part of the plate denotes the east.

According to Gemelli[44] the south was denoted by a "blue field," and the symbol Tochtli; east by a red field, and the symbol Acatl; the north by a "yellow field," and the symbol Tecpatl, and the west by a "green field," and the symbol Calli. In this plate we have precisely the colors he mentions, red in the east, and yellow in the north, but green is at the south, and blue at the west.

Sahagun remarks[45] that "at the end of fifty-two years the count came back to *Cetochtliacatl* (one-Rabbit-Cane), which is the figure of the reed dedicated to the east, which they called *Tlapeopcopa* and *Tlavilcopa*, nearly towards the fire or sun."[46]

This language is peculiar and important, and indicates that he had a Mexican painting similar to the plate now under discussion before him, in which the year symbols were at the *corners* instead of at the *sides*. On this supposition only can we understand his use of the term "*Cetochtli-acatl*," and the expression "nearly towards the fire," &c. His use of the term "fire" in this connection undoubtedly indicates red. His language is therefore in entire harmony with what we find on this plate.

According to Gemelli and Chavero the element *earth* was assigned to the south; in this plate, in the right space inclosed by the green loop, we see the great open jaws representing the earth out of which the tree arises. From a careful examination of this figure, so frequently found in this and other Mexican Codices, I am convinced it is used as the symbol of the grave and of the earth. The presence of this symbol and of the figure of death in this space, as also the figures of the gods of death and the under world in the corresponding space of the Cortesian plate,

---

[44] l. c.   See also the colored wheel in Kingsborough, Mex. Antiq., Vol. IV.   Copied from one in Boturini's collection, the same as Gemelli's.

[45] l. c.

[46] Y acabados los cincuenta y dos años tornaba la cuenta á cetocltliacatl, que es la caña figura dedicada al oriente que llamaban tlapcopcopa, y tlavilcopa, casibacia la lumbre, ó al sol.

strongly inclined me for a time to believe that this should be considered the north, as in the Aztec superstitions one class of the dead was located in that region; but a more thorough study leads me to the conclusion that these figures are intended to represent the earth and to symbolize the fact that here is to be found the point where the old cycle ends and the new begins. I will refer to this again when I return to the description of the Cortesian plate.

All the authorities, except Boturini, refer the year Tecpatl or Flint to the north, which agrees with the theory I am advancing, and in the lower left-hand corner we find in the red circle the figure of a flint, which according to my arrangement applies to the north, represented by the yellow loop.

How, then, are we to account for the presence of this symbol on the head of the right figure in the red or eastern loop? Veytia says, "They (the Mexicans) gave to fire the first place as the most noble of all (the elements), and symbolized it by the flint." This I acknowledge presents a difficulty that I am unable to account for only on the supposition that this author has misinterpreted his authorities, for no one so far as I can find gives the "sun" or "age of fire" as the first, the only difference in this respect being as to whether the "sun of water" or the "sun of earth" was first. This difference I am inclined to believe (though without a thorough examination of the subject) arises chiefly from a variation of the cardinal point with which they commence the count, those starting at the south commencing with the element earth, those beginning at the east with water.[a] Not that the authors themselves always indicated these points, but that a proper interpretation of the original authorities would have resulted in this conclusion, supposing a proper adjustment of the different calendar systems of the Nahua nations to have been made. I think it quite probable that the artist who painted this plate of the Fejervary Codex believed the first "sun" or "age" should be assigned to the east, and that here the flint indicates origin, first creative power or that out of which the first creation issued, an idea which I believe is consonant with Nahua traditions. I may as well state here as elsewhere that notwithstanding the statement made by Gemelli and others that it was the belief or tradition of the Mexicans that the sun first appeared in the south, I am somewhat skeptical on this point.

Such a tradition might be possible in an extreme northern country, but it is impossible to conceive how it would have originated in a tropical region.

The calendar and religious observances were the great and all absorbing topics of the Nahua nations, and hence it is to these, and especially the first, that we must look for an explanation of their paintings and

[a] See the various views presented by Chavero, *Anales Mus. Mex.* Tom. II Entrag. 2, and authorities referred to by Bancroft, *Native Races*, II. p. 504, note 3.

sculpture, and not so much to the traditions given by the old Spanish authors.

Finally, the assignment of the year symbols to the four points at which we find them was not, as these early authors supposed, because of their significance, but because in forming the circle of the days they fell at these points. This fact is so apparent from the plates of the Codices that it seems to me to forbid any other conclusion.

In the bottom, blue loop, which we call the west, we see two female figures, one of them with cross-bones on her dress. This agrees precisely with the statement of Sahagun heretofore given, to wit, "for they held the opinion that the dead women, who are goddesses, live in the west, and that the dead men, who are in the house of the sun, guide him from the east with rejoicings every day, until they arrive at midday, and that the defunct women, whom they regard as goddesses and call Cioapipiltin, come out from the west to receive him at midday (or south?), and carry him with rejoicing to the west." Before comparing with the plate of the Cortesian Codex, we call attention to some other plates of the Mexican Codices, in order to see how far our interpretation of the plates of the Fejervary Codex will be borne out.

Turning now to Plates 65 and 66 of the Vatican Codex B [a] (shown in our Plate IV), we observe four trees (or crosses) each with an individual clasping the trunk. One of these individuals is red, the other white, with slender red stripes and with the face black, another green, and the other black. On the top of each tree, except the one at the right, is a bird ; on the right tree, or rather broad-leaved tropical plant, which is clasped by the black individual, is the figure of the tiger or rabbit. As these are probably intended to represent the seasons (spring, summer, &c.), the ages, or the years, and consequently the cardinal points, let us see with what parts of the plate of the Fejervary Codex they respectively correspond.

By turning back to page 50 the reader will see that the days of the first column, viz, Cipactli, Coatl, &c., or numbers 1, 5, 9, 13, 17 were referred to the east, the second column 2, 6, 8, 12, 16 to the north, &c. Each of the four trees has below it, in a line, five day characters. Below the fourth one are Xochitl, Malinalli, Cuetzpalin, Cozcaquauhtli, and Tochtli, precisely those of the fourth column, and which, in accordance with our interpretation of the Fejervary Codex, are assigned to the south.

Referring to the first or left-hand of these four groups, we observe that the clasping figure is red, and that the days in the line underneath are 1, 5, 9, 13, 17, those of the east, agreeing in all respects with our interpretation of the Fejervary plate.

The days below the second group, with the white and red striped individual, are 2, 6, 10, 14, 18, indicating the north, and those below the third, with the green individual, 3, 7, 11, 15, 19, denoting the west.

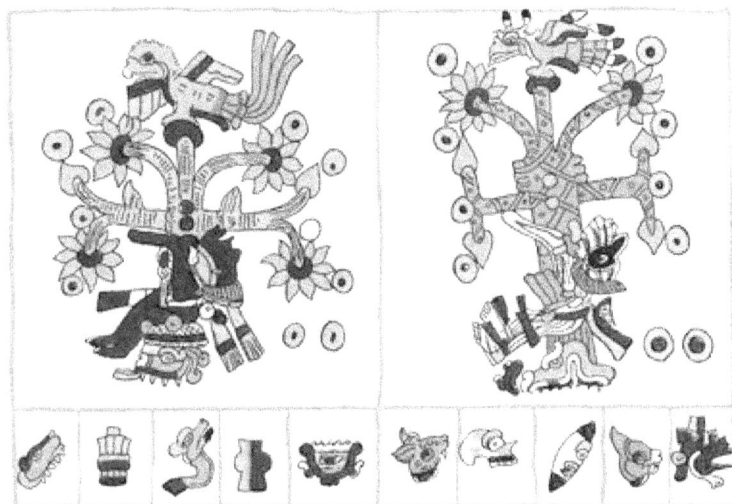

COPY OF PLATE 65, VATICAN CODEX, B

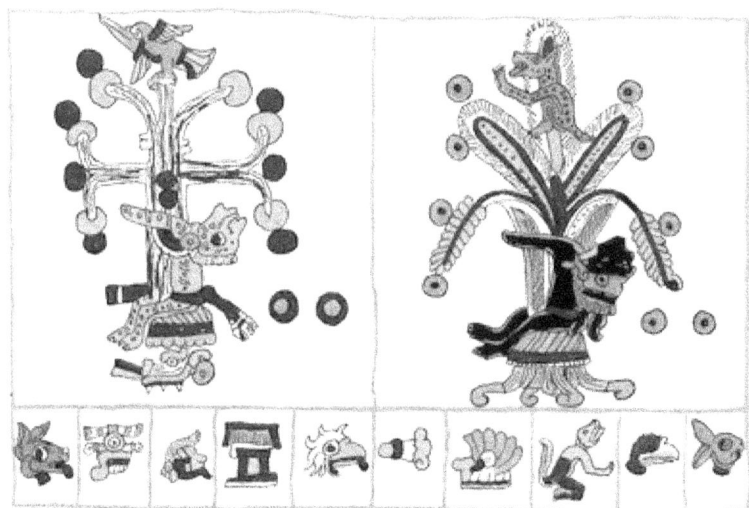

COPY OF PLATE 66, VATICAN CODEX, B

So far the agreement with our theory of the other plate is perfect, but in this case we have taken the figures from the left to the right, this being, as we have seen in the *Tonalamatl*, or table of days, copied from this Codex, the direction in which they are to be read when in a line.

We notice also that the bird over the first tree, although differing in some respects from it, is the same as that in the top or red loop of the other plate, and that over the third tree the same as that in the blue or bottom loop, agreeing also in this respect.

From these facts we understand that the black figure is sometimes at least assigned to the south.

I am fully aware of the difficulties to be met with in attempting to carry out this assignment of colors, in explanation of other plates of this and other Codices, nor do I believe colors can be relied upon. They form some aid in the few plates of general application to the calendar, and where there are reasons, as in the cases given, to suppose the cardinal points will be indicated in some regular order. The same thing is true also in regard to the Manuscript Troano. For example, if we suppose character *a* of Fig. 7 to denote the east, *b* north, *c* west, and *d* south, we shall find them arranged in the following different ways:

c	*b*		*a b c d*	*c d a b*	*c*	*a*
d	*a*				*d*	*b*
a	*d*				*c*	*d*
c	*b*				*a*	*b*

Combine with these colors and other distinctive marks, then vary them in proportion, and we should have an endless variety, just as we see in the Mexican Codices. We can only hope to solve the problem, therefore, by selecting, after careful study, those plates which appear to have the symbols arranged in their normal order.

Turning to plate 43 of the Borgian Codex, we find it impossible to make it agree, either with the plate of the Fejervary Codex or the Vatican Codex. Here we find the days 1, 5, 9, 13, 17 associated with the green figure in the lower left-hand square; 2, 6, 10, 14, 18 with the yellow figure in the lower right-hand square; 3, 7, 11, 15, and 19 with the black figure in the upper right-hand square, and 4, 8, 12, 16, 20 with the red figure in the upper left-hand square. What adds to the difficulty is the fact that the symbol of the *Cane* accompanies the black figure, thus apparently indicating that this denotes the year Acatl. That these groups are to be taken in the same order as those of Plate 44 of the Fejervary Codex, that is around to the left, opposite the sun's course, is evident from the days and also from Plate 9 of this (Borgian) Codex, where the twenty days of the month are placed in a circle.

In this latter the order of the four years is indicated by the first days of the years, viz, *Cipactli, Miquiztli, Ozomatli,* and *Cozcaquauhtli* placed in blue circles at the corners in the following order:

Ozomatli.	Miquiztli.
Cozcaquauhtli.	Cipactli.

In the lower right-hand corner of Plate 4, same Codex, is a square with the four quadrants very distinctly colored and arranged thus:

Yellow.	Green.
Blue	Red.

and a large red circle in the center, on the body of what is evidently intended as a symbol of *Cipactli.* As this appears to be a figure of general application, we presume that it commences with *Cipactli,* the day on which the cycles began. As the four names of the days with which the years began probably show, as arranged in the above square, their respective positions in the calendar wheel, I infer that, in their normal arrangement, *Cipactli* corresponded with the red, *Miquiztli* with the green, *Ozomatli* with the yellow, and *Cozcaquauhtli* with the blue. This brings the colors in precise accordance with those on the cross in the lower right-hand square of Plate 43; and if we suppose the black figure to correspond with the blue it brings the colors in the same order, but the day groups are shifted around one point to the left. It is probable therefore that this plate, like a number of others in the same Codex, is intended to denote the relation of colors and day groups to each other in some other than the first or normal year, or possibly to the seasons or the four Indications of the cycle.

But be this as it may, I do not think the difficulty in reconciling the arrangement of the colors and days in this Codex will warrant the rejection of our explanation of the plates of the other codices. That Plate 44 of the Fejervary Codex is one of general application must be admitted, as is also the "Table of the Bacabs" from the Cortesian Codex; and if the true assignment to the cardinal points is made anywhere it will certainly be in these. Turning now to the latter, as shown in our Plate II, where the erased characters are restored, we note the following facts, and then with some general remarks conclude our paper, as we have no intention of entering upon a general discussion of the Mexican Calendar, which would be necessary if we undertook to explain fully even the plates of the codices we have referred to.

As before remarked, the Cortesian plate is arranged upon the same plan as that of the Fejervary Codex, evidently based upon the same theory and intended for the same purpose. In the latter the four year symbols are placed in the outer looped line at the four corners, and so distinguished as to justify us in believing they mark their respective quadrants. In the former we find the four Maya year-bearers, Cauac, Kan, Muluc, Ix, in corresponding positions, each distinguished by the numeral character for 1 (see 31, 1, 11, and 21 in our scheme, Fig. 2), the first, or the right, corresponding with the green loop and the year Tochtli; the second, at the top, corresponding with the red loop and the year Acatl; the third, at the left, corresponding with the yellow loop and the year Tecpatl, and the fourth, at the bottom, corresponding with the blue loop and the year Calli. This brings Cauac to the south, Kan to the east, Muluc to the north, and Ix to the west, and the correspondence is complete, except as to the colors, which, as we have seen, cannot possibly be brought into harmony. This view is further sustained by the fact that the god of death is found on the right of each plate, not for the purpose of indicating the supposed abode of the dead, but to mark the point at which the cycles close, which is more fully expressed in the Cortesian plate by piercing or dividing the body of a victim with a flint knife [a] marked with the symbol of Ezanab (the last day of the Ix years) and the symbol of Ymix, with which, in some way not yet understood, the counting of the cycles began.

In the quotation already made from Sahagun we find the following statement: "Tecpatl, which is the figure of a flint, was dedicated to *Mictlampa*, nearly towards hell, because they believed that the dead went towards the north. For which reason, in the superstition which represented the dead as covered with mantas (cloths) and their bodies bound, they made them sit with their faces turned toward the north or *Mictlampa*."

Although he is referring to Mexican customs, yet it is worthy of note that in this Cortesian plate there is a sitting unmummied figure, bound with cords, in the left space, which, according to my interpretation, is at the north side.

Since the foregoing was written I have received from Dr. D. G. Brin

---

[a] Dr. Brinton, "The Maya Chronicles," p. 53, informs us that "the division of the katuns was on the principle of the Beltran system of numeration, as *xel u ca katun*, 'thirty years;' *xel u yox katun*, 'fifty years.' Literally these expressions are, 'dividing the second katun,' 'dividing the third katun,' *xel* meaning to cut to pieces, *to divide as with a knife*." This appears to be the idea intended in the figure of the Cortesian plate.

ton a photo lithograph of the "wheel of the Ah-cuch-haab" found in the book of Chilan Balam, which he has kindly allowed me to use. This is shown in Fig. 9.

Fig. 9.—Calendar wheel from book of Chilan Balam.

In this (smaller circle) we see that Kan is placed at the top of the cross, denominated *Lakin*, or east ; Cauac at the right, *Nohol*, or south ; Mulue at the left, *Xaman*, or north ; and Hiix at the bottom, *Chikin*, or west.

Although this shows the marks of Spanish or foreign influence, yet it affords corroborative evidence of the correctness of the view advanced. The upper and larger circle is retained only to show that the reading was around to the left, as in the Cortesian plate.

This result of our investigations, I repeat, forces us to the conclusion that *a*, Fig. 7, is the symbol for east, as stated in my former work, *b* of north, *c* of west, and *d* of south.

Among the important results growing out of, and deductions to be drawn from, my discovery in regard to these two plates, I may mention the following :

First. That the order in which the groups and characters are to be taken is around to the left, opposite the course of the sun, which tallies with most of the authorities, and in reference to the Maya calendar confirms Perez's statement, heretofore mentioned.

Second. That the cross, as has been generally supposed, was used among these nations as a symbol of the cardinal points.

Third. It tends to confirm the belief that the bird figures were used to denote the winds. This fact also enables us to give a signification to the birds' heads on the engraved shells found in the mounds of the United States, a full and interesting account of which is given by Mr. Holmes in a paper published in the Second Annual Report of the Bureau of Ethnology.[56] Take for example the three shells figured on Plate LIX—reproduced in our Fig. 10—Nos. 1, 2 and 3. Here is in each case the four-looped circle corresponding with the four loops of the Cortesian and Fejervary plates, also with the looped serpent of the Mexican calendar stone, and the four serpents of Plate 43 of the Borgian Codex. The four bird heads on each shell are pointed toward the left, just as on Plate 44 of the Fejervary Codex, and Plates 65 and 66 of the Vatican Codex B, and doubtless have the same signification in the former as in the latter—the *four winds*, or winds of the four cardinal points. If this supposition be correct, of which there is scarcely room for a doubt, it not only confirms Mr. Holmes's suggestions, but also indicates that the mound builders followed the same custom in this respect as the Nahua nations, and renders it quite probable that there was more or less intercourse between the two peoples, which will enable us to account for the presence in the mounds of certain articles, which otherwise appear as anomalies.

Fourth. Another and more important result is the proof it furnishes of an intimate relation of the Maya with the Nahua nations. That all the Central American nations had calendars substantially the same in principle as the Mexican, is well known. This of itself would indicate a common origin not so very remote ; but when we see two contiguous or neighboring peoples making use of the same conventional signs of a complicated nature, down even to the most minute details, and those of a character not comprehensible by the commonalty, we have proof at least of a very intimate relation. I cannot attempt in this place to discuss the question of the identity or non-identity of the Maya, Toltec and Aztec nations, nor the relations of one to the other, but follow the usual method, and speak of the three as distinct.

---

[56] P. 281, pl. 69.

FIG. 15.—Engraved shells from mounds.

If Leon y Gama is correct in his statement,[*] " No todos comenzaban
á contar el circlo por un mismo año ; los Toltecos lo empezaban desde
Tecpatl ; los de Teotihuacan desde *Calli* ; los Mexicanos desde *Tochtli* ;
y los Tezcocanos desde *Acatl*," and the years began with *Cipactli*, we
are probably justified in concluding that the Fejervary Codex is a
Tezcucan manuscript.

Be this as it may, we have in these two plates the evidence of an intimate relation between the Maya and Nahua nations, as that of the
Cortesian Codex certainly appertains to the former and the Fejervary
as certainly to the latter.

Which was the original and which the copy is a question of still
greater importance, as its proper determination may have the effect to
overturn certain opinions which have been long entertained and generally conceded as correct. If an examination should prove that the
Mayas have borrowed from the Nahuas it would result in proving the
calendar and sculptures of the former to be much more recent than has
been generally supposed.

It must be admitted that the Mexican or Nahua manuscripts have
little or nothing in them that could have been borrowed from the Maya
manuscripts or inscriptions ; hence, if we find in the latter anything
belonging to or found in the former it will indicate that they are borrowed and that the Mexican are the older.

In addition to the close resemblance of these two plates, the following
facts bearing upon this question are worthy of notice. In the lower
part of Plate 52 of the Dresden Codex we see precisely the same figure
as that used by the Mexicans as the symbol of *Cipactli*.

The chief character of the hieroglyphic, 15 R. (Rau's scheme), of the
Palenque Tablet is a serpent's head (shown correctly only on the stone in
the Smithsonian Museum and in Dr. Rau's photograph), and nearly the
same as the symbol for the same Mexican day. The method of representing a house in the Maya manuscripts is substantially the same as
the Mexican symbol for *Calli* (House). The cross on the Palenque
Tablet has so many features in common with those in the blue and red
loops of the Fejervary Codex as to induce the belief that they were derived from the same type. We see in that of the Tablet the reptile
head as at the base of the cross in the blue loop, the nodes, and probably the bird of that in the red loop, and the two human figures.

What is perhaps still more significant, is the fact that in this plate of
the Fejervary Codex, and elsewhere in the same Codex, we see evidences
of a transition from pictorial symbols to conventional characters ; for example, the yellow heart shaped symbol in the lower left-hand corner of the
Fejervary plate which is there used to denote the day *Ocelotl* (Tiger). On
the other hand we find in the manuscript Troano for example, on plate
III, one of the symbols used in the *Tonalamatl* of the Vatican Codex
B and in other Mexican codices to signify water. On Plate XXV* of

_____

[*] Dos Piedras, pt. 1, p. 16.

the same manuscript, under the four symbols of the cardinal points, we see four figures, one a sitting figure similar to the middle one with black head, on the left side of the Cortesian plate; one a spotted dog sitting on what is apparently part of the carapace of a tortoise; one a monkey, and the other a bird with a hooked bill. Is it not possible that we have here an indication of the four days—Dragon, Death, Monkey, Vulture, with which the Mexican years began?

In all the Maya manuscripts we find the custom of using heads as symbols, almost, if not quite, as often as in the Mexican codices. Not only so, but in the former, even in the purely conventional characters, we see evidences of a desire to turn every one possible into the figure of a head, a fact still more apparent in the monumental inscriptions.

Turning to the ruins of Copan as represented by Stephens and others, we find on the altars and elsewhere the same death's-head with huge incisors so common in Mexico, and on the statues the snake-skin so often repeated on those of Mexico. Here we find the *Cipactli* as a huge crocodile head,[32] also the monkey's head used as a hieroglyphic.[33]

The pendant lip or lolling tongue, which ever it be, of the central figure of the Mexican calendar stone is found also in the central figure of the sun tablet of Palenque[34] and a dozen times over in the inscriptions.

The long, elephantine, Tlaloc nose, so often repeated in the Mexican codices, is even more common and more elaborate in the Maya manuscripts and sculptures, and, as we learn from a Ms. paper by Mr. Gustav Eisen, lately received by the Smithsonian Institution, has also been found at Copan.

Many more points or items of agreement might be pointed out, but these will suffice to show that one must have borrowed from the other, for it is impossible that isolated civilizations should have produced such identical results in details even down to conventional figures. Again we ask the question, Which was the borrower? We hesitate to accept what seems to be the legitimate conclusion to be drawn from these facts, as it compels us to take issue with the view almost universally held. One thing is apparent, viz, that the Mexican symbols could never have grown out of the Maya hieroglyphics. That the latter might have grown out of the former is not impossible.

If we accept the theory that there was a Toltec nation preceding the advent of the Aztec, which, when broken up and driven out of Mexico,

---

[32] Travels in Cent. Amer., vol. I, p. 156. Monument N, plate. Mr. Gustav Eisen, in a Ms. lately received by and now in possession of the Smithsonian Institution, also mentions another similar head as found at Copan. This, he says, is on the side of an altar similar to that described by Stephens, except that the top wants the hieroglyphics. The sides have human figures similar to the other; on one of these is the head of an "Alligator."

[33] Ibid., 2d plate to p. 155.

[34] Stephens' Trav. Cent. Amer. III Frontispiece.

proceeded southward, where probably colonies from the main stock had already been planted, we may be able to solve the enigma.

If this people were, as is generally supposed, the leaders in Mexican and Central American civilization, it is possible that the Aztecs, a more savage and barbarous people, borrowed their civilization from the former, and, having less tendency toward development, retained the original symbols and figures of the former, adding only ornamentation and details, but not advancing to any great extent toward a written language.

Some such supposition as this, I believe, is absolutely necessary to explain the facts mentioned. But even this will compel us to admit that the monuments of Yucatan and Copan are of much more recent date than has generally been supposed, and such I am inclined to believe is the fact. At any rate, I think I may fairly claim, without rendering myself chargeable with egotism, that my discovery in regard to the two plates so frequently mentioned will throw some additional light on this vexed question.

NOTE.— Since the foregoing was printed, my attention has been called by Dr. Brinton to the fact that the passage quoted from Sahagun (see pages 41 and 54), as given in Bustamente's edition, from which it was taken, is incorrect in combining *Cetochtli* and *Acatl* into one word, when in fact the first is the end of one sentence and the second the commencement of another. I find, by reference to the passage as given in Kingsborough, the evidence of this erroneous reading. The argument on page 54, so far as based upon this incorrect reading, must fall.